Ready-to-Use Interventions for
Elementary and Secondary Students with
Attention Deficit Hyperactivity Disorder

Problem Solver Guide
for Students with
ADHD

Harvey C. Parker, Ph.D.

Specialty Press, Inc.
300 N.W. 70th Ave.
Plantation, Florida 33317

ISBN 1-886941-29-7

Library of Congress Cataloging-in-Publication Data
Parker, Harvey C.
    Problem solver guide for students with ADHD: ready-to-use interven-
tions for elementary and secondary students with attention deficit
hyperactivity disorder/Harvey C. Parker.
        p. cm.
    Includes bibliographical references and index.
    ISBN 1-886941-29-7 (alk. paper)
    1. Attention-deficit-disordered children--Education--Handbooks, manuals,
    etc. 2. Attention-deficit-disordered youth--education--manuals, etc. 3.
    Attention-deficit hyperactivity disorder--Handbooks, manuals, etc. I.Title

    LC4713.2 .P27 2000
    371.93--dc21   00-058370

Cover Design by Redemske Graphic Designs

10 9 8 7 6 5 4 3 2 1

Printed in the United States of America

Specialty Press, Inc.
300 Northwest 70th Avenue, Suite 102
Plantation, Florida 33317
(954) 792-8100 • (800) 233-9273
www.addwarehouse.com

Dedication

To Francine Fisher.
Her courage and strength will always be an
inspiration to those who knew her.

Table of Contents

Chapter 1

A Quick Look at ADHD

Introduction

This book was designed to be used as a quick reference guide for parents and teachers of elementary and secondary school students with attention-deficit/hyperactivity disorder (ADHD). Much has been written on the subject of teaching and raising children and adolescents with ADHD, however, there are few books which provide lists of practical strategies. The strategies contained in this book come from the actual experiences of educators, parents, and clinicians who work with ADHD children and adolescents.

This chapter provides a quick look at ADHD. Next are chapters which contain strategies teachers and parents can use to help students with academic weaknesses, behavior problems, inattention, other psychological problems, social skills deficits, and poor study habits. Later chapters contain information on medications to treat ADHD and federal laws which protect the rights of disabled students.

Students with ADHD typically experience a great deal of difficulty in school. Problems with inattention, hyperactivity, or impulsivity can affect learning, behavior, and social and emotional adjustment. Their teachers often report that they rush through work, pay little attention to instructions or details, exhibit disruptive behavior, don't complete homework, and lag behind socially.

In response to these problems parents and teachers may try a number of interventions. Close monitoring of schoolwork provides structure for the student. Additional help in subject areas where the student needs assistance may remediate weaknesses in reading, math, or language skills. Accommodations provided by teach-

1

ers in class such as shorter assignments, closer supervision, untimed tests, and seating in quiet areas can also help.

Many children with ADHD are identified in elementary school. Those who are very hyperactive and impulsive will be noticed early because their social behavior is inappropriate. They often cannot follow rules, have difficulty staying quiet, and have trouble getting along with other children. Those who are not hyperactive, but who have problems only in the area of attention span, are usually identified later because assignments are not completed and they have trouble keeping up.

By the time children with ADHD get to secondary school they are less likely to admit to needing help. Schools are less likely to offer help and parents may not be as able to help the student with middle or high school level school work. Problems often increase. Grades fall and school becomes a losing battle. Without intervention the downward spiral often continues.

What's the Big Deal About ADHD Anyway?

It seems like everybody these days is talking about ADHD. Some people say kids and parents are just using it as an excuse for their child's poor school work and bad behavior. Others are worried that too many children are being diagnosed and too many are given drugs to control their behavior. The media has made a considerable effort to inform the public about ADHD. Unfortunately, not all of the information depicting ADHD which you read about in newspapers and magazines or watch on television is accurate.

What is the big deal about having ADHD anyway? Is it such a huge problem? What causes ADHD? What happens to kids with ADHD when they get older? These are some of the questions that will be answered in this chapter.

What is ADHD?

ADHD affects a child's ability to regulate behavior and attention. Students with ADHD often have problems sustaining attention, controlling hyperactivity, and managing impulses.

Although we can easily regulate many things in our environment, regulating ourselves is not always so simple. We control an air conditioner by lowering or raising the temperature on a thermostat. We slow down a car by releasing the pressure on the accelerator. We enter numbers on a panel to control the cooking time or heat intensity of a microwave oven. We use a remote control to lower the volume of a television set. Switches, pedals, panels, or buttons make regulation of these devices simple.

However, people don't have switches, pedals, panel or buttons for regulating their attention and behavior. If we did, perhaps ADHD would not exist. Unfortunately, the process of self-regulation–purposefully controlling behavior–is rather complicated. The brain is responsible for self-regulation–planning, organizing, and carrying out complex behavior. These are called "executive functions" of the brain. They develop from birth through childhood. During this time, we develop language to communicate with others and with ourselves, memory to recall events, a sense of time to comprehend the concept of past and future, visualization to keep things in mind, and other skills that enable us to regulate our behavior. Executive functions are carried out in an area of the brain called the orbital-frontal cortex. This part of the brain may not be as active in people with ADHD.

Difficulties in self-regulation exist to some degree in everyone. Many people have experienced problems with concentration. Sometimes it's a result of being tired, bored, hungry, or distracted by something. We have all had times when we were overly restless or hyperactive. Times when we couldn't sit still and pay attention, became overly impatient, or too easily excited, and too quick to respond. Does this mean we all have ADHD? No. although problems with self-regulation are found in everyone from time to time, these problems are far more likely to occur in people with ADHD. And they lead to significant impairment in one's ability to function at home, in school, at work, or in social situations.

How Common is ADHD?

Most experts agree that ADHD affects from 5 to 7 percent of the population. Children with ADHD have been identified in every country in which ADHD has been studied. For example, rates of ADHD in New Zealand ranged in several studies from 2 to 6 percent, in Germany 8.7 percent, in Japan 7.7 percent, and in China 8.9 percent.

ADHD is not a new disorder. Pediatricians, psychologists, psychiatrists, and neurologists have been diagnosing and treating children and adolescents with ADHD for dozens of years. In fact, almost half the referrals to mental health practitioners in schools, clinics, or private practices are to treat children and adolescents who have problems related to inattention, hyperactivity, or impulsivity.

ADHD is more common in boys than girls. Girls are often older than boys by the time they are diagnosed and they are less likely to be referred for treatment. This is because the behavior of girls with ADHD is not usually disruptive or aggressive. Girls are typically less trouble to their parents and teachers.

What Causes ADHD?

ADHD has been extensively studied for more than fifty years. With recent advances in technology which allows us to study brain structure and functioning there has been a greater appreciation for the neurobiological basis of ADHD. Studies involving molecular genetics have provided us with mounting evidence to support the theory that ADHD can be a genetic disorder for many individuals. But not everyone who has ADHD inherited it. ADHD may also be caused by problems in development related to pregnancy and delivery, early childhood illness, head injury caused by trauma, or exposure to certain toxic substances.

How is ADHD Diagnosed?

A physician or mental health professional with appropriate training can diagnose children suspected of having ADHD. This generally includes pediatricians, psychiatrists, neurologists, family practitioners, clinical psychologists, school psychologists, social workers, and other mental health professionals. Training and experience in working with children with ADHD may vary substantially among individuals in each of these professional disciplines.

The Diagnostic and Statistical Manual of Mental Disorders, Fourth Edition, Text Revision (DSM IV-TR), published by the American Psychiatric Association in 2000, provides health care professionals with the criteria that need to be met to diagnose a person with ADHD. To receive a diagnosis of ADHD a person must exhibit a certain number of behavioral characteristics reflecting either inattention or hyperactivity and impulsivity for at least six months to a degree that is "maladaptive and inconsistent with developmental level." These behavioral characteristics must have begun prior to age seven, must be evident in two or more settings (home, school, work, community), and must not be due to any other mental disorder such as a mood disorder, anxiety, learning disability, etc. These characteristics are listed below:

Inattention Symptoms
    a. often fails to give close attention to details or makes careless mistakes in schoolwork, work, or other activities
    b. often has difficulty sustaining attention in tasks or play activities
    c. often does not seem to listen when spoken to directly
    d. often does not follow through on instructions and fails to finish schoolwork, chores, or duties in the workplace (not due to oppositional behavior or failure to understand instructions)
    e. often has difficulty organizing tasks and activities
    f. often avoids, dislikes, or is reluctant to engage in tasks that require sustained mental effort (such as schoolwork or homework)
    g. often loses things necessary for tasks or activities (e.g., toys, school assignments, pencils, books, or tools)
    h. is often easily distracted by extraneous stimuli
    i. is often forgetful in daily activities

Hyperactive Symptoms

a. often fidgets with hands or feet or squirms in seat
b. often leaves seat in classroom or in other situations in which remaining seated is expected
c. often runs about or climbs excessively in situations in which it is inappropriate (in adolescents or adults, may be limited to subjective feelings of restlessness)
d. often has difficulty playing or engaging in leisure activities quietly
e. is often "on the go" or often acts as if "driven by a motor"
f. often talks excessively

Impulsive Symptoms

g. often blurts out answers before questions have been completed
h. often has difficulty awaiting his or her turn
i. often interrupts or intrudes on others (e.g., butts into conversations or games)

There are three types of ADHD. Some children with ADHD show symptoms of inattention and are not hyperactive or impulsive. Others only show symptoms of hyperactivity-impulsivity. Most, however, show symptoms of *both* inattention and hyperactivity-impulsivity.

• predominantly inattentive type
• predominantly hyperactive-impulsive type
• combined type

While the term ADHD is the technically correct term for either of the three types indicated above, in the past the term attention deficit disorder (ADD) was used, and still is by many. For the past ten years ADD and ADHD have been used synonymously in publications and in public policy.

Complete This ADHD Symptom Checklist

Below is a checklist containing 18 items which describe characteristics frequently found in people with ADHD. Items 1-9 describe characteristics of inattention. Items 10-15 describe characteristics of hyperactivity. Items 16-18 describe characteristics of impulsivity.

In the space before each statement put the number that best describes your child's (your student's) behavior (0=never or rarely; 1 = sometimes; 2 = often; 3 = very often).

____ 1. Fails to give close attention to details or makes careless mistakes in schoolwork, work, or other activities.

____ 2. Has difficulty sustaining attention in tasks or play activities.

____ 3. Does not seem to listen when spoken to directly.

____ 4. Does not follow through on instructions and fails to finish schoolwork, chores, or duties in the workplace (not due to oppositional behavior or failure to understand instructions).

____ 5. Has difficulty organizing tasks and activities.

____ 6. Avoids, dislikes, or is reluctant to engage in tasks that require sustained mental effort (such as schoolwork or homework).

____ 7. Loses things necessary for tasks or activities (e.g., toys, school assignments, pencils, books, or tools).

____ 8. Is easily distracted by extraneous stimuli.

____ 9. Is often forgetful in daily activities.

____10. Fidgets with hands or feet or squirms in seat.

____11. Leaves seat in classroom or in other situations in which remaining seated is expected.

____12. Runs about or climbs excessively in situations in which it is inappropriate (in adolescents or adults, may be limited to subjective feelings of restlessness).

____13. Has difficulty playing or engaging in leisure activities quietly.

____14. Is "on the go" or often acts as if "driven by a motor."

____15. Talks excessively.

7

___16. Blurts out answers before questions have been completed
___17. Has difficulty awaiting his or her turn.
___18. Interrupts or intrudes on others (e.g., butts into conversations or games).

Count the number of items in each group (inattention items 1-9 and hyperactivity-impulsivity items 10-18) you marked "2" or "3." If six or more items are marked "2" or "3" in each group this could indicate serious problems in the groups marked.

How is ADHD Treated?

Fortunately, we have made many advances in treating ADHD. Pharmaceutical companies have developed new medications to manage symptoms. A number of medications have withstood the scrutiny of years of scientific study. Their safety and effectiveness has been well documented.

Educators understand the importance of providing assistance to children and adolescents with ADHD in school. Public schools are now required to provide special education and related services to students with ADHD who need such assistance. Schools must also meet the needs of those with ADHD who require accommodations in regular education classes. Such programs may "even the playing field" for those disabled by ADHD who must compete with other students in school.

Families benefit from national support groups such as Children and Adults with Attention Deficit Hyperactivity Disorder (CHADD) and the National Attention Deficit Disorder Association (ADDA). Information on behavior management, social skills training, and ways to raise a child or teen with ADHD is readily available in books, videos, and on the Internet.

What Happens to Kids with ADHD When They Grow Up?

Unfortunately, having ADHD can have a major impact on the course of a student's education and career attainment. Students with ADHD are more likely to be suspended from school, less likely to earn grades as high as non-ADHD students, less likely to attend and complete college, and less likely to attain as much success in their careers. With early intervention and treatment these disappointing outcomes could be improved.

Look for Warning Signs of Trouble in School

When a student develops a problem in school, early detection and rapid intervention are desirable. Parents often find out too late when their son or daughter is having trouble. Teachers may not notice a student who is struggling. Look for the early warning signs listed below.

✓ frequently complains about being bored in school
✓ has excessive absenteeism
✓ has a recent drop in grades
✓ lacks interest in homework
✓ has problems with tardiness
✓ talks about dropping out of school
✓ expresses resentment toward teachers
✓ rarely brings books or papers to or from school
✓ gets reports from teachers that the student is not completing work
✓ shows significant signs of disorganization (i.e., books and papers not appropriately cared for)
✓ does work sloppily or incorrectly
✓ has an "I don't care" attitude about school
✓ has low self-esteem
✓ gets complaints from teachers that he/she is inattentive
✓ has trouble completing homework
✓ has school projects that are not complete or missing
✓ exhibits hyperactivity which interferes with learning
✓ fails to do assigned work in class
✓ hangs out with other students who are not doing well in school
✓ has trouble comprehending assignments when trying to do them
✓ has unauthorized absences from school

We should be concerned if a student is exhibiting even one or two of these warning signs. This could be the beginning of a downward spiral. Rarely do students turn this negative cycle around without help or intervention from parents or teachers.

Summary

The purpose of this book is to provide teachers and parents with a quick reference guide to strategies that can be used to help children with ADHD. ADHD is a fairly common problem which affects up around 5 percent of children and adolescents.

Students with ADHD often exhibit signs of inattention, hyperactivity, and impulsivity. This causes them to have such problems as organizing and completing work, sustaining attention on tasks, controlling behavior, and adjusting socially in school and elsewhere. Learning disabilities and other psychological disorders are commonly found in children with ADHD. Early identification and intervention may be very helpful.

Chapter 2

Strategies to Help
with Academic Skill Problems

Students with ADHD have a greater risk of having academic skill problems. These problems could be the result of different factors. For example, difficulty with attention and focus will obviously cause the student to miss important instruction. Insufficient practice and review of material taught in class will reduce the chance of strengthening skills. Deficits in speech and language or in perceptual processing (such as auditory or visual memory, association, or discrimination) may be more common in students with ADHD. Such deficits are often associated with problems in learning.

Unexpected difficulty in learning to read and spell is often called dyslexia. Unexpected means that there is no obvious reason for the difficulty, such as inadequate schooling, auditory or visual sensory problems, acquired brain damage, or low overall IQ. Dyslexia is a prevalent disorder, affecting as many as 20 percent of the population.

Both genetic and environmental factors can cause dyslexia. Current evidence supports the view that dyslexia is a familial disorder (about one third of first degree relatives are affected). It also has a high degree of heritability (about 50 percent). Environmental factors such as large family size and low socioeconomic status (SES) may contribute to reading problems. Some lower SES families read less to their children, play fewer language games with them, and children in such families may lack sufficient preschool experiences to accelerate growth in reading and language development. Early exposure to language enrichment activities may be a very important factor in developing later reading and language skills.

Below are strategies teachers and parents can use to help students who have problems in reading, written or oral language, and mathematics.

Strategies for Problems with Reading—Decoding and Comprehension

• In young children look for early signs which can be precursors to reading or spelling problems: speech delay, articulation difficulty, problems learning letter names or color names, word-finding problems, missequencing syllables ("aminals" for "animals," "donimoes" for "dominoes"), and problems remembering addresses, phone numbers, and other verbal sequences.

• Other signs to look for in a student with language or potential reading problems is difficulty following directions, reduced speech or difficulty expressing ones self, and problems with peer relations. Language problems can interfere with a child's ability to express emotions. The child may be more likely to act out his feelings physically or withdraw from social interaction.

• The single most important step to overcome a reading problem is for the child to receive individualized tutoring in a phonics-based approach to reading. Being able to sound out words is so central to reading development that it cannot be bypassed even if the student has difficulty with this process. While whole language approaches to reading may work well with non-dyslexic youngsters, such approaches do not help dyslexic youngsters. They need much more sustained and systematic instruction in phonological coding. Some examples of programs that use a phonics approach and which teach letter-sound relations and blending are the Orton Gillingham, Slingerland, and DISTAR aproaches.

- It is also quite important to teach students skills involved in reading comprehension. An important reading comprehension skill is learning the meaning of words and how to use them correctly. Building an extensive reading vocabulary should be the goal of every teacher and parent for every student across all grades. The most effective way to increase a student's vocabulary is to introduce new words. Parents tend to do this naturally. When a child hears a new word he will often ask its meaning. Provide definitions and use the new word in a sentence. Continue to use the new word in the days to follow so the child has continued exposure to it.

- Teachers and parents can build vocabulary by using visual imagery. For example, if you were trying to teach the meaning of the word "apex" you might create an index card with an image of an ape standing on the top of a mountain or on the top of the letter "X".

APEX
Definition:
highest point

Sentence:
An ape climbed to the
apex of the mountain.

Note: from Leslie Davis, Sandi Sirotowitz, and Harvey C. Parker (1996). *Study Strategies Made Easy*. Florida: Specialty Press, Inc. Copyright 1996 by Leslie Davis and Sandi Sirotowitz. Reprinted with permission

- We can increase the size and depth of a student's vocabulary by teaching the meanings of the most common prefixes and suffixes.

- Reduce over-reliance on common words by teaching synonyms and antonyms.

- Provide additional reading time. Use "previewing" strategies. Select text with less on a page. Shorten amount of required reading. Avoid oral reading. Allow use of "Cliff Notes" to gain an understanding of subject matter prior to reading the complete document. Use books on tape to assist in comprehension of book. Use highlighters to emphasize important information in a reading selection.

- Students with reading problems may prefer to subvocalize when reading silently. Recitation of the reading selection aloud (but quietly) may enable them to better attend to and recall information read. If you observe students doing this, allow them to continue as the additional auditory input may be helping them.

- Poor readers often focus on decoding more than comprehension. They may not be actively focusing on the meaning of what they are reading. Teachers can help by introducing main concepts of the reading selection beforehand, thereby providing contextual clues to the poor reader.

- Even students with ADHD who have excellent decoding skills and who can read fluently will have trouble maintaining their concentration while reading. They often report having to reread material due to lapses in concentration. Focus may be improved by shortening the length of reading assignments; pausing and asking questions of the student; encouraging the student to take short notes while reading; or listing questions the student should try to answer while reading before the reading begins. Note, that these strategies are geared to encourage the student to be an "active" reader as opposed to a "passive" reader. Active reading may help the student keep focused on the task at hand.

- Introduce new vocabulary words or difficult concepts found in a reading selection ahead of time so the student will be better able to read the material with fluency and understanding.

- Make sure the material being read by the student is at the student's independent reading level—material the student is capable of reading successfully on his own.

- A student who has trouble with visual tracking may lose his place easily while reading. Use of a tracking device such the Reading Helper™ which contains a clear window that goes over a line of type can help the student maintain his place while reading. This is available from the A.D.D. WareHouse—(800) 233-9273.

- If a reading selection is too long or too difficult for the student, have others in the class read the material out loud (either taking turns or as a whole class) to help ease the burden.

- The teacher could read the selection to the student as the student follows along. After reading a few paragraphs have the student read back what was covered.

- Assign a "reading partner" to a student who is weak in reading. The student and his partner can take turns reading paragraphs or pages. By partnering, students can help one another with decoding words, answering questions, and understanding the content of the material read.

- Provide time each day (15-20 minutes) for students to do free choice reading. Encourage building a class library of books students enjoy. Have students make recommendations of certain books to others. Start a reader's club and award points to students who read.

- Perhaps the most effective strategy to improve reading comprehension is previewing by the teacher. In previewing, the teacher summarizes key points of the material to be read in the same sequence as they appear in the reading selection. Unfamiliar words should also be previewed to reduce decoding and comprehension problems.

- Teachers can improve reading comprehension by asking students questions before reading rather than after reading. Pre-reading questions alert readers to what the writer wants them to know.

- Teach students how to find the main idea of paragraphs and to identify sub-ideas.

- Have the student paraphrase (describe in his own words) the main ideas and sub-ideas of a reading selection. The ability to paraphrase is critical for success in both reading and writing.

- Use the strategy of reciprocal teaching to improve reading comprehension. Pair children off in the classroom and have one teach the other what has been learned from reading a selection. Start by having each child read the material and make up a few questions about the content that could be asked to the other child.

- Teach outlining so the student can practice picking out the main idea and sub-ideas.

- Teach students how authors construct textbooks. The purpose of chapters, headings, subheadings, print that is bolded, italicized, or underlined, side-boxes, illustrations, charts, captions, etc.

- Have the student highlight important ideas in the reading selection on a photocopied sample.

- Teach the SQ3R technique of reading comprehension. This involves the following steps:
    1. Survey—briefly review the reading selection. Scan the titles, headings, subheadings, and read the chapter summary.

    2. Question—rephrase the headings and subheadings of a selection into questions.

    3. Read—read the material and ask yourself questions about the selection, (i.e., What is the main idea of this paragraph?).

    4. Recite—paraphrase the meaning of what you have read.

    5. Review—after reading, review the selection once again by scanning and checking to see how much you remember and understood.

- Parents have important roles to play in the treatment of their dyslexic child. They serve as advocates and sources of emotional support. Although parents may serve the role as tutor for children who do not have serious reading and language problems it may be inadvisable for them to assume such a role if their child is significantly dyslexic. For one, they do not have the proper training. Secondly, the parent-child tutoring relationship can negatively affect the normal relationship the parent and child should have in the course of their family life.

- Reading is a fundamental skill that is learned and practiced both inside and outside the classroom. Parents play an important role in the development of reading and language skills. Parents should make sure that their child sees them read often and write letters, messages, and instructions. Showing their child they read and write often, sends a powerful message to the child.

- Parents should be encouraged to help their child find reading material that is of interest to the child. This makes the reading process easier. If the child is a sports fan, for instance, locate books, magazines, or articles in the newspaper that fit this interest. If fashion is what catches your child's eye, find books on this topic. Parents and teachers should encourage recreational reading.

- Among the unproven treatments for dyslexia or reading problems are the visual therapies: convergence training, eye movement exercises, colored lenses, and devices to induce "peripheral" reading. Medications intended to affect vestibular system functioning have not proved to be helpful. Chiropractic, megavitamins, and dietary treatments have also not been shown to be helpful.

Strategies for Problems with Spelling and Written or Oral Expression

- In the past twenty years the approach to instruction in written language has changed. Today there is more emphasis on the use of writing to express and communicate ideas than on the mechanics of writing—handwriting, punctuation, spelling, etc. Writing involves a process of thinking, planning, composing, revising, editing, and sharing ideas. Teach these five steps for writing papers.

1. Teach pre-writing as the first step in writing. The purpose of this step is to think about ideas to write about. Help the student select a topic and talk about the topic with the student. Encourage the student to brainstorm ideas and make note of them on paper. Use these notes to form a list of what he wants to write about in some sequential order.

2. The second step of the writing process involves writing a first draft. Stress content rather than spelling, penmanship, or grammar.

3. The third step is revising. Acknowledge the student's efforts in the first draft and build on these efforts together by discussing additional ideas or changes that could be made to the work product.

4. The fourth step is editing. The teacher directs attention to grammar, spelling, punctuation, capitalization, and word usage. Encourage the student to use the COPS method to check his work. COPS stands for:

   C Capitalization—check for capitalization of first words in sentences and proper nouns.

   O Overall appearance of work—check for neatness, margins, paragraph indentation, complete sentences.

   P Punctuation—check for commas and appropriate punctuation at end of sentences.

   S Spelling—check to see all words are spelled correctly.

5. The fifth step is publishing. The student should make a final copy of the work to share with others.

- For some children writing can be such a grueling chore the teacher should be willing to accept non-written forms for reports (i.e. displays, oral, projects). Accept use of a typewriter, a word processor, or a tape recorder. Do not assign large quantity of written work. When possible, test with multiple choice or fill-in questions.

- Students with ADHD may have more difficulty with spelling. They may not pay attention to detail when writing or may be careless. This can cause spelling errors. Some students may have weaknesses in auditory or visual memory which can also contribute to problems with spelling.

- If spelling is weak: allow use of Franklin Spellers (headphone if speller talks), a dictionary, or other spell check tools.

- Encourage the student to play games such as Scrabble™, Hangman™, and Boggle™ to encourage focus on how words are spelled.

- Teach a phonetic approach to word analysis. Although many words are not spelled as they sound, a good understanding of phonics can be a powerful aid to weak spellers. Help the student find little words within the word and show the student how to break words into syllables.

- Encourage the student to keep track of his most often misspelled words. These words can be collected on a list or on index cards and put in a card file. The word should be written on the front of the card and the meaning on the back for new words.

- Overlook spelling errors when appropriate on assignments where spelling is not the focus of the assignment.

- If spelling is a diagnosed disability, disregard misspellings when grading.

- Students with ADHD often have difficulty with fine-motor control. This can affect their handwriting. For some, written work becomes so laborious they avoid it. Writing assignments that may take other students a few minutes, may take the student with fine-motor problems hours to complete.

- Encourage the student to use a sharp pencil and have an eraser available.

- Teach appropriate posture and how to position the paper correctly.

- Experiment with pencil grip, special papers, etc.

- Allow student to use laminated handwriting cards, containing samples of properly formed letters.

- Explain to the student that he will have a better chance of getting good grades if his work is done neatly. Help the student improve the legibility of his work by teaching him to evaluate the quality of his handwriting. In their book, *Overcoming Underachieving*, Sam Goldstein and Nancy Mather encourage students to use the acronym PRINT to check their work:
  P Proper letter formation?
  R Right amount of spacing between letters and words?
  I Indented paragraphs?
  N Neatness?
  T Tall letters above the middle line, short letters below?

- Permit the student in the upper grades to print rather than use cursive writing if this is a struggle for him.

- Stress the importance of neatness and organization in written assignments. Provide guidelines of how you expect papers to be written. Encourage the use of headings on papers, use of specific formats, etc.

- Permit the student to tape record assignments as opposed to writing.

- Reduce the amount of written work required. Stress accuracy rather than amount.

- Although it is very important to continue to help students with motor coordination problems to write legibly, many can benefit from learning keyboarding skills so they can use a word processor.

- For secondary students who take classes which require a great deal of note taking, have another student make a photocopy of his notes.

- Allow the student to dictate an assignment to another student or a parent or sibling at home.

- If oral expression is weak: accept all oral responses, substitute display for oral report, encourage expression of new ideas or experiences, pick topics that are easy for the student to talk about.

Strategies for Problems with Mathematics

Over the past decade schools have changed the focus of the math curriculum. There has been a shift from paper and pencil computation to activities which require mathematical reasoning and problem solving. To teach these skills, math teachers must stimulate students to learn in a different way. Students are encouraged to observe and experience their world and use these observations and experiences to solve problems involving mathematical concepts. Although it remains important for students to learn to add, subtract, multiply, and divide, they will also need to learn to use calculators, computers, and thinking skills to problem solve.

- For young children, provide instruction in telling time. Begin by making sure the child can recognize numbers from 1 to 12 on the face of a clock or watch. The child must be able to count by ones and fives to 60 and to differentiate the hour hand from the minute hand on a clock or watch. Move from the simple to the complex by first teaching how to tell time on the hour, then the half hour, then the quarter hour, and then by minutes. Teach the different ways that people express times before and after certain hours. For example, 9:30 can be described as "nine-thirty," "half past nine," or "thirty minutes to the hour." Go over other phrases which describe time such as "almost ten," "five past nine," "a quarter past four," etc.

- Teach or reinforce concepts associated with money. Counting money and making change correctly are important life skills. Children need to be able to estimate costs. Children with math weaknesses often have trouble in this area. Begin by teaching the value of coins and bills. Use play money from a Monopoly™ game or real currency. Encourage counting money out loud and adding to amounts to come up with new totals. Give the child the opportunity to make change, make purchases in stores, etc.

- Children need to learn concepts of measurement. This involves measuring objects, liquids, solids, and being able

23

to read fractional parts of an inch on a ruler. To help the child with measurement of liquids or solids encourage the child to follow recipes that include measurement terms. Have the child work with a ruler to measure length and to read temperatures from a thermometer.

- Understanding the concept of directions and the vocabulary associated with describing different directions is an important concept for children to learn.

- Review math vocabulary frequently.

- Give sample problems and provide clear explanations on how to solve them. Permit use of these during tests.

- Encourage student to estimate answers prior to calculating problems.

- Allow use of calculators when appropriate.

- Some students will make careless math errors when calculating because they are not able to line up figures correctly on paper. Encourage these students to use graph paper to space numbers evenly.

- Provide additional time to complete assignments for students who are weak in math. By reducing time pressure the student may have more time to check work.

- Provide immediate feedback and instruction via modeling of the correct computational procedure. Teach the steps needed to solve a particular type of math problem. Give clues to the process needed to solve problems and encourage use of "self-talk" to proceed through problem-solving.

- Reduce the number of math problems assigned.

- Reduce the amount of copying needed to work math problems from a text book by supplying photocopied work sheets.

- Provide models of sample problems.

- Teach signal words in a math problem that tell the process to be used to solve the problem. For example, words such as "plus," "sum," and "together" indicate addition; words such as "product," "times," and " doubled" indicate multiplication; words such as "quotient," " parts," " average," and " sharing" all indicate division.

Summary

Academic skill problems in areas related to reading, spelling, handwriting, and mathematics can be found in students with ADHD. Reading comprehension deficits may be due to problems with decoding, poor language comprehension, short attention span, rushing through reading selections, forgetfulness, or other difficulties. Strategies for decoding words through a phonics-linguistic approach, previewing, peer partnering, outlining, vocabulary building, and many others can be very helpful with dyslexic students.

Students with ADHD may also have problems with handwriting, spelling, and organization of written work. Accommodations can be very helpful, but strategies should also be taught to improve legibility of the student's writing.

Problems in learning mathematical concepts and in doing math work neatly and accurately can be a significant factor for students with ADHD. Lack of close attention to detail, carelessness in writing and solving problems, and other problems in mathematics can be helped through the use of appropriate strategies described in this chapter.

Chapter 3

Strategies to Help
with Behavior
and Academic Performance

Performing in school successfully and getting along well with peers requires self-control. This is something students with ADHD (particularly the hyperactive-impulsive type) have in short supply. They often exhibit behavior which can seriously disrupt the classroom. Below is a list of common behavior problems found in students with ADHD:

✓ calling out in class
✓ interrupting others
✓ not waiting his/her turn
✓ excessive hyperactivity or restlessness
✓ not listening when spoken to directly
✓ losing things necessary for tasks or activities
✓ poor organization
✓ excessive loudness or noisiness
✓ talking excessively
✓ losing temper easily; easily frustrated
✓ bossy; trouble getting along with peers
✓ arguing with adults or peers

Teachers have found that students with these behavior problems do best in situations where:

1. expectations and rules are clear;
2. there is close monitoring and supervision;
3. activities, tasks, and lessons have high interest to students; and

4. both positive and negative feedback about behavior is provided.

Many of the strategies listed in this chapter provide ways for the teacher to incorporate these four qualities in the classroom.

- **Post class/school rules** in a conspicuous place. Clearly communicated rules are helpful in maintaining proper classroom decorum. Students with ADHD may need such rules to be reviewed daily. When possible, consequences for rule violations should be specified.

- **Be alert to early warning signs** of a problem. Anticipate trouble brewing. Intervene quickly before a situation becomes problematic.

- Provide concrete, visual examples of appropriate and inappropriate behavior. Use **role-playing** to illustrate these behaviors giving students clear guidelines as to teacher expectations.

- Establish **routines** for regular classroom activities such as handing out and collecting papers, entering and leaving the room, taking attendance, answering questions, etc.

- Remind students of what you expect in terms of behavior and learning before starting an activity or lesson.

- Use **"proximity control"** to manage problem behavior. Stay near the student who is acting out so you can provide immediate, frequent praise for appropriate behavior and quickly intervene when/if negative behavior occurs.

- **Redirect** the acting out student to more appropriate behavior when you notice inappropriate behavior (i.e., a student who is talking to another student could be redirected to get on task).

- Praise positive behavior often. Positive reinforcement is an effective way to motivate students to behave appropriately. Use of verbal praise can be extremely effective. Some students prefer quiet, private praise while others prefer public praise.

Sample Compliments

Great job!	Way to go!
You made it look easy.	Now you're cookin'!
Good thinking!	Keep up the good work!
Fantastic!	I like your style.
I knew you could do it.	You learn quickly.
That's terrific!	I'm proud of you.
That's good.	Outstanding!
Keep at it.	Good for you.
Right on!	Couldn't be better.
That's right!	Good answer.
You got it!	Perfect!
You keep improving.	That was great!
Sensational!	Looking great.
Nice try.	Much better!

- Change rewards or punishments that have little effect on behavior. Ask the student what types of rewards he or she would be motivated to earn or what negative consequences would the student be motivated to avoid.

Suggested School Rewards

Being teacher's helper.	Being first in line.
Erasing chalkboard.	Pick from "toy box"
Free time with friend.	Homework pass.
Sitting near a friend.	Stickers.
Running an errand.	Extra recess time.
Grading papers.	Playing a game.
Classroom monitor.	Taking care of animals.
Writing on chalkboard.	Field trip.

Getting award certificate. Lunch with teacher.
Getting better grade. Removal of poor grade.
Positive note to parents. Collecting papers.

- Use **response-cost** to encourage behavior change. Response cost (loss of tokens or points, privileges, free time, etc.) should be implemented for student misbehavior. Behavior change is most effective when teachers praise or reward positive behavior and provide punishment (response costs) for inappropriate student behavior.

- Provide **immediate feedback** about behavior. Behavior of students with ADHD is modified best when feedback is provided at the "point of performance" and not several minutes, hours, or even days later. Positive and negative feedback following behavior is a powerful change motivator. Positive reinforcement strengthens appropriate behavior while punishment will weaken inappropriate behavior. Teachers should be alert to opportunities to reinforce "good" behavior and should apply such reinforcement quickly. Similarly, negative behavior should be addressed immediately.

- **Ignore** minor inappropriate behavior. Reacting to small occurrences of inappropriate behavior may actually cause the behavior to increase. A more effective strategy would be to ignore the misbehavior and praise an incompatible positive behavior. For example, a student with ADHD who has trouble controlling the impulse to call out an answer may be helped by ignoring called out answers and praising the student for raising her hand.

- **Use teacher attention** to praise positive behavior. Teacher attention is by far the most powerful behavior management tool a teacher has in the classroom. Use it wisely to motivate students.

- Use **"prudent" reprimands** for misbehavior. A prudent reprimand is one which directs the student to stop inappropriate behavior without causing shame, embarrassment, or unnecessary attention. Imprudent reprimands contain unnecessary lectures, threats, belittling remarks, etc.

- **Supervise** closely during transition times. Winding down from one activity and winding up for another can be difficult for students with ADHD. Those who are hyperactive and impulsive may have particular difficulty stopping a train of thought or action. Behavior may perseverate, especially if it is exciting (i.e., settling down to work after lunch, P.E., etc.). Those who are inattentive may have difficulty getting energized for a new activity. Monitor the behavior of all students with ADHD during transitions and provide appropriate motivation for them to stop and start new types of activity.

- Seat student near good role models. Insulate the student from distractions by seating him close to students who are attentive and responsible.

- Set up **behavior contracts**. Contracts provide a system to both motivate and remind the student to behave in an expected way. Contracts should contain one to five attainable goals which should be reviewed daily by the teacher and student. A menu of reinforcers should be constructed with the student to be provided in-class by the teacher or at home by the parent. Below are some examples of behavior that can be improved with behavior contracts:
  ✓ tardiness to class
  ✓ incomplete homework

31

✓ talking out of turn
✓ talking without permission
✓ rudeness to other students or to teacher
✓ not paying attention to a lessons
✓ failure to complete in-class assignments
✓ moving about the room without permission

- Write a **behavior plan** to modify the student's behavior. For example, if during a small group reading lesson, a student talks and disrupts others use the questions below to construct a behavior plan.
  1. What is the behavior I want the student to stop?
  2. How often does this behavior occur?
  3. What is the appropriate (target) behavior that I would like the student to exhibit?
  4. How many times or for how long should I expect the student to exhibit the target behavior to earn a reward?
  5. What reward (privilege or activity) would the student like to earn?
  6. When will the reward be given?

- Establish a **classroom token economy system**. A token economy system is a form of behavioral contracting which uses tokens as an immediate reward for certain behavior or task performance. Follow these steps when setting up a classroom token economy system.
  1. Explain the concept of a token economy system to the student.
  2. Select an appropriate token such as points, poker chips, fake money, etc.
  3. List two to five START behaviors targeted for improvement on a daily or weekly chart. Make sure the target behaviors are positively phrased and described in a way which is observable and measurable.
  4. Assign a token value for each behavior.

CLASSROOM TOKEN ECONOMY SYSTEM

START BEHAVIORS	Value	M	T	W	Th	F

STOP BEHAVIORS	Value	M	T	W	Th	F

REWARDS	Value	M	T	W	Th	F
TOTAL TOKENS REMAINING						

5. Fines can be a part of the token system as well. Select a few STOP behaviors which are problematic and remove tokens when those behaviors are displayed. The judicious use of fines can be effective in discouraging inappropriate behavior.

6. Determine rewards for which the tokens can be exchanged and make a reward menu from which the student could choose, i.e., a favorite activity, free time, no homework pass, food, run errand, etc.

7. Decide when tokens will be given and when they might be exchanged for rewards. Generally speaking, when starting a new program, try to reward new target behaviors frequently by administering tokens often and by offering the student frequent opportunities to cash-in the tokens for rewards.

8. Construct a daily or weekly chart on which the target START and STOP behaviors will be listed along with their respective token value.

9. Praise success and encourage better performance in weak areas. Maintain a positive, encouraging attitude.

•   Dr. Michael Gordon invented the *Attention Training System (ATS)* to be used along with a classroom token economy to help motivate students to pay attention. The ATS is a small electronic counter which is placed on the student's desk. The ATS automatically awards the child a point every sixty seconds. If the student wanders off task, the teacher uses a remote control to deduct a point and activate a small warning light on the student's module. Points earned on the ATS may be exchanged for rewards or free time activities within the token economy system.

The *Attention Training System (ATS)* has been used in schools throughout the country. It can be ordered through

Gordon Systems, Inc. or through the A.D.D. WareHouse (800) 233-9273.

• Set up a **home and school-based contingency program** such as the Goal Card Program described below. Home and school-based contingency programs involve the collaboration between school and home in the assessment of student behavior by the teacher, and the administration of rewards and consequences at home, based upon the teacher's assessment. The program is similar to a token economy system described earlier. Parents of ADHD students, used to working with teachers, quickly adapt to the home-based contingency program and often appreciate having daily feedback as to their child's school performance. Daily reporting generally facilitates better parent-teacher communication and encourages the development of home-school partnerships. Parents don't have to wait for parent-teacher conferences or report cards to learn about their child's progress.

Use daily report cards like the Goal Card Program is quite common for students with ADHD. The immediate feedback provided by the teacher and opportunity to earn rewards at home and at school can be a great incentive for students.

How To Use the Goal Card Program

The Goal Card Program, useful for children in grades one through eight, is a home and school-based contingency program which targets five behaviors commonly found to be problematic for ADHD children in the classroom. There are two forms of the program: a single rating card on which the child is evaluated once per day each day for the entire week and a multiple rating card on which the child is evaluated several times per day either by subject, activity, period, or teacher.

35

Child's Name_____ Grade_____

Teacher_____ School_____

Week of _____ Days of the Week (or subjects/periods/teachers per day)

GOAL CARD	MON	TUE	WED	THU	FRI
1. Paid attention in class					
2. Completed work in class					
3. Completed homework					
4. Was well behaved					
5. Desk and notebook neat					
TOTALS					
Teacher's Initials					

N/A = not applicable

0=losing, forgetting or
    destroying the card

1 = Poor   4 = Good

2 = Needs Improvement 5 = Excellent

3 = Fair

Teacher's Comments

_____

_____

_____

Parent's Comments

_____

_____

_____

Most children in elementary school will be able to use a single rating Goal Card because they will be evaluated by one teacher one time per day. Those elementary school students who require more frequent daily ratings, due to high rates of inappropriate behavior, or because they are evaluated by more than one teachere each day, will need a multiple rating card scored by subjects or periods. Middle school students, who usually have several teachers in one day, will need to use the multiple rating card.

Regardless of whether the child is evaluated one or more times a day the target behaviors can remain the same and may include:
• Paid Attention
• Completed Work
• Completed Homework
• Was Well Behaved
• Desk and Notebook Neat

The student is rated on a five point scale (1=Poor, 2=Improved, 3=Fair, 4=Good, 5=Excellent). When a category of behavior does not apply for the student for that day, e.g. no homework assigned, the teacher marks N/A and the student is automatically awarded 5 points.

STEP 1: Explaining the Program to the Child

1. The child is instructed to give the Goal Card to his teacher(s) each day for scoring.
2. The teacher(s) scores the card, initials it and returns it to the student to bring home to his parents for review.
3. Each evening the parents review the total points earned for the day. If the child is using the single rating Goal Card, it is to be brought to school each day for the rest of the week to be completed by the teacher. If a multiple rating Goal Card is used, then the child should be given a new card to bring to school for use the following day.
4. It is important that a combination of rewards and consequences be utilized since ADD children are noted to have a high reinforcement tolerance. That is, they seem to require larger reinforcers and stronger consequences than non-ADHD children.
5. Explain to the child that if he forgets, loses, or destroys the Goal Card he is given zero points for the day and appropriate consequences should follow.

STEP 2: Setting Up Rewards and Consequences

When using the Goal Card Program be careful to set your reinforcement and punishment cut-off scores at a realistic level so that the child can be successful on the card provided that he is making a reasonable effort in school. Although individual differences need to be considered, we have found that a Goal Card score of 17 points or more per day is an effective cut-off score for starting the program.

As the child improves in performance, the cut-off score can be raised a little at a time in accordance with the child's progress. If the child receives less than the cut-off number of points on any given day then a mild punishment (e.g. removal of a privilege, earlier bed time, etc.) should be provided. For points at or above the amount expected, a reward should be forthcoming.

Constructing a List of Rewards

The child and parents should construct a list of rewards which the child would like to receive for bringing home a good Goal Card. Some sample rewards are:

- additional time for television after homework
- staying up later than usual
- time on video game
- a trip to the store for ice-cream, etc.
- playing a game with mom or dad
- going to a friend's house after school
- earning money to buy something or to add to savings
- exchanging points for tokens to save up for a larger reward

Constructing a List of Negative Consequences

The child and parents should construct a list of negative con-sequences one of which could be imposed upon the child for failure to earn a specified number of points on the Goal Card. Negative consequences should be applied judiciously given consideration for the ADD student's inherent difficulties. Some examples are:

- early bedtime for not reaching a set number of points
- missing dessert
- reduction in length of play time or television time
- removal of video game for the day

STEP 3: Using the Program

During the first three days of the program, baseline data should be collected. This is the breaking-in phase wherein points earned by the student will count toward rewards, but not to-ward loss of privileges. As with any new procedure, it is likely that either the child or teacher will occasionally forget to have the Goal Card completed. Such mistakes should be overlooked during this breaking-in phase.

After this brief period it is essential that the teacher score the Goal Card daily. The teacher should ask the child for the card even when the child forgets to bring it up for scoring and should reinforce the child for remembering on his own to hand in the card for scoring. If the child repeatedly does not bring the card to the teacher for scoring the teacher should explain the importance of daily review of the card to the child. A mild consequence may be applied if the child continues to forget the card.

Generally the best time to score the card for elementary school students who are on a single rating system is at the end of the day. Middle school students, of course, should obtain scores after each period. Ignore any arguing or negotiating on the part of the student regarding points earned. Simply encourage the child to try harder the next day.

Parents should be certain to review the Goal Card on a nightly basis. It is not wise to review the card immediately upon seeing the child that afternoon or evening. Set some time aside before dinner to review the card thoroughly and dispense appropriate rewards or remove privileges if necessary. After reviewing the card parents should use a monthly calendar to record points earned each day for that month.

• Instruct student in **self-monitoring**. In self-monitoring, children are trained to observe specific aspects of their behavior or academic performance and to record their observations. For example, a student may be asked to observe whenever he calls out without raising his hand, whenever he is off-task when a signal is heard, or whether he was disruptive during a transition from say PE back to the classroom.

When designing a self-monitoring program the teacher will need to explain to the child the what, when, and how of self-monitoring.
1. What behavior is to be observed.
2. When the student should do the observation (usually to a specific signal or prompt by the teacher or automatic device, but sometimes the student is trained to self-prompt or note their behavior on their own from time to time).
3. How the student should record the observation.

The most popular recording devices in school settings are paper-and-pencil forms. These can range from index cards to slips of paper on which the child makes a tally mark when prompted. The form may be taped to the student's desk, included in the student's work folder, or carried by the student from class to class. The *Student Planbook* of the ADAPT Program (Attention deficit Accommodation Plan for Teaching) by Harvey C. Parker, Ph.D. contains a number of self-monitoring forms.

The form below was designed to remind students to proofread written work. The student is taught to check his work by answering each questions.

Proofreading Checklist

Name:_____   Date:_____

After you have finished your writing assignment, check your work for neatness, spelling, and organization. Circle either YES or NO.

Assignment:_____

Heading on paper?...YES	NO
Margins correct?..YES	NO
Proper spacing between words?............................ YES	NO
Handwriting neat?.. YES	NO
Sentences start with capital letters?.......................YES	NO
Sentences end with correct punctuation?................YES	NO
Crossed out mistakes with only one line?.............. YES	NO
Spelling is correct?... YES	NO

The form below was designed to be used with an audio cassette tape that beeps at variable intervals ranging from 30 to 90 seconds. The beep serves as a prompt for the student to mark on the self-monitoring form if he was paying attention to his work when the beep sounded. The student circles "yes" or "no." The *Listen, Look and Think Program* (Parker, 1990), which includes an endless cassette "beep" tape and self-monitoring forms, can be ordered through the A.D.D. WareHouse (800) 233-9273.

Was I Paying Attention?

Name:_____ Date:_____

INSTRUCTIONS
Listen to the beep tape * as you do your work. Whenever you hear a beep, stop working for a moment and ask yourself, "Was I paying attention?" Circle your answer and go right back to work. Answer the questions on the bottom of the page when you finish.

Was I Paying Attention?

YES	NO
YES	NO
YES	NO
YES	NO
YES	NO
YES	NO
YES	NO
YES	NO
YES	NO
YES	NO
YES	NO
YES	NO
YES	NO
YES	NO
YES	NO
YES	NO

Did I follow the directions?	Yes	No
Did I pay attention?	Yes	No
Did I finish my work?	Yes	No
Did I check my answers?	Yes	No

If the goal is to improve the productivity of the student, the following self-monitoring form could be used. For those students who are slow, but accurate in their work there may be no need to have them record the number of

41

problems done correctly. Determine the number of minutes for each work period and have a timer signal the end
of the period when the student should count the number
of problems completed.

How Much Work Did I Do?

Time Period	# Problems Completed	# Problems Correct
1.	_____	_____
2.	_____	_____
3.	_____	_____
4.	_____	_____
5.	_____	_____
6.	_____	_____
7.	_____	_____
8.	_____	_____
9.	_____	_____
10.	_____	_____
11.	_____	_____
12.	_____	_____
13.	_____	_____
14.	_____	_____
15.	_____	_____

When using self-monitoring programs it is important that
the teacher determine the accuracy of students' self-monitoring.

• Encourage parental cooperation and support of teacher.
Frequent communication between school and home is
often quite important to maintain appropriate classroom
behavior of students, especially young students. Daily or
weekly home notes, phone conversations, or e-mailing
will help all parties stay informed about the student's behavior. Close collaboration between home and school
can lead to the development of successful behavior plans.

- Identify the cause of behavior problems. Not all problem behavior of students with ADHD will be the result of their ADHD. For example, many other factors can cause students to have behavior problems. Poor understanding of assigned work, anxiety, low self-esteem, lack of motivation, a learning disability, or other factors can lead to behavior problems.

- Maintain a calm, firm voice when directing students. Teachers who use assertive styles of communication tend to be more successful in maintaining control of their classroom.

- Move around the room frequently to provide appropriate supervision of all students, but stay in closer proximity to disruptive students.

- If student appears depressed, try talking with the child to better understand her feelings. Refer the child to a counselor for further assessment if necessary.

- Watch for situations or events that trigger misbehavior. Such triggers are antecedent events and if they can be prevented the associated misbehavior will often disappear as well.

- Arrange for a parent-teacher-student conference.

- Many students with ADHD take medication to help with attention and self-control. There are many types of medications that can be prescribed to students. Which medication a doctor will prescribed will depend on the doctor's experience with the medication, the student's needs, and the response to the medication. Response is difficult to predict and doctors will often rely on teacher evaluations of the student's performance in school to determine appropriate medication and dosing. Teachers may be asked to provide oral or written reports to the doctor or parent. Completing rating scales is a good way to monitor medication effects and side effects. When trying a new medication, teacher reports may be required weekly and then with less frequency once the appropriate medication and proper dosing has been established.

- Change the student's seat.

- Establish location where student could "chill out."

- For an active student, allow the student to stand sometimes while working. The student who is hyperactive may have trouble staying seated for a length of time. Give the student permission to stand near her desk or work in an area of the room where her movement would not distract others.

- Provide opportunity for "seat breaks."

- Provide short breaks between assignments. Avoid presenting lessons back-to-back that involve close attention to detail or highly repetitive, boring tasks. Follow one of these lessons with a more active lesson which encourages student participation, class discussion, or movement in the classroom.

- Give extra time to complete tasks. Fidgety, active students may need more time to work on tasks because they may not be able to settle down to work and complete seatwork as quickly as others.

Interventions for Students Who Talk Excessively

- Establish clear rules in the classroom as to when talking to others is acceptable and when it is not. Some students may not be able to distinguish when talking is appropriate, particularly if the teacher maintains a cooperative work environment where students work together to complete projects.

- Discuss with the talkative student why talking is inappropriate at certain times. Explain that excessive talking disturbs others and interferes with the student's ability to complete work.

- At the beginning of a lesson give the student a signal when it is time to be quiet. Signals may include an index finger up against your lips, red and green papers posted to indicate times when it is OK to start conversations and appropriate to end them, or a statement to the entire class that this is time for listening, not talking.

- Establish a consequence for unacceptable talking and apply the consequence consistently to all students who break the "no talking" rule. Suggested consequences are name on the board, time-out in a section of the classroom for five minutes, loss of time from recess, etc.

- If you notice a student talking, first try to reinforce a nearby student for working quietly.

- If the student continues to talk, issue a warning to stop.

- If the student stops and then continues, act right away by providing a consequence. Remember to use negative consequences judiciously with students who have ADHD. Always emphasize the use of positive approaches first for changing behavior.

Interventions for Students Who Call Out

- Students call out for a variety of reasons. Some are so impulsive that whenever they get excited or frustrated, everyone has to know about it. For these children, over-arousal is difficult to suppress and they act out verbally or physically. Students with ADHD are particularly prone to overreact to excitement or disappointment. During transition times from unstructured to structured activities, impulsive children will have a difficult time settling down.

- During transition from one activity to another, let students know what is expected of them Emphasize the use of hand raising to ask permission to talk.

- Ignore students who call out without raising their hand and asking permission to talk.

- Verbally praise students who raise their hands before talking.

- Quickly call on students who have raised their hands.

- Positively acknowledge hand raising behavior by such remarks as, "Jim, you've raised your hand, what is the answer?"

Interventions for Students Who Turn in Sloppy Work

- Students turn in sloppy work for a variety of reasons. They may not take pride in their performance or expect too little from themselves. Some students want to get their work finished as quickly as possible regardless of whether or not it is done correctly. Some students have developed poor work habits. Past teachers may have accepted substandard papers. Evaluate the reason a student is turning in sloppy work and initiate an appropriate strategy from those listed below.

- Establish clear guidelines for neatness.
  a. Proper heading should be on all work.
  b. Papers should not be crumpled.
  c. Ink should not be smeared.
  d. Writing should be done in one style, not part cursive and part printing.
  e. Mistakes should be erased if done in pencil and crossed out once if done in ink.
  f. Letters should be sized and spaced evenly.
  g. Handwriting should be slanted in one, consistent direction.
  h. Handwriting should stay on the lines and within proper margins.
  i. Misspellings should be corrected.
  j. Proper capitalization and punctuation should be used.

- Reinforce the student's attempts at neatness.

- Return papers that are not done neatly. Expect them to be done over unless the student has a fine-motor impairment which accounts for illegibility or sloppiness. In such cases, consider training in the use of computer keyboarding skills or occupational therapy to improve motor control.

- Use a self-monitoring procedure to encourage neatness. Find four samples of the student's work which vary from neat to sloppy. Ask the student to rate the four samples (Best, Good, Fair, and Poor) and put ratings on the top of each paper. Laminate these samples and have the student keep them in a notebook for reference. Encourage the student to use the neatest sample as an example of how all future work should be done. Have the student compare the neatness of any new work to the quality of the work of each of the four examples (see self-monitoring ideas discussed earlier and in previous chapter).

- Provide encouragement to students whose neatness is improving.

- . For elementary students, display examples of neat work to other members of the class.

Strategies for Teachers to Manage Their Own Stress and Frustration

- Take a deep breath and relax when the ADHD student is acting out.

- Try not to overreact to misbehavior. Stay calm and consider appropriate consequences.

- Think ADHD—not BAD! Consider the underlying reasons for the student's behavior and take the appropriate steps to handle it professionally.

- Ask for support from other school faculty and staff when needed.

- Be flexible and try to keep your sense of humor.

Summary

Student with ADHD frequently have problems with behavior and academic performance in school. Inattention, hyperactivity, and impulsivity can result in the student calling out in class, interrupting others, not waiting his or her turn, not listening to instructions, losing things necessary for tasks, being poorly organized, talking excessively, etc. Teachers can institute a number of behavior management strategies to correct these problems. Contracts, in-class contingency management programs, daily home notes, self-monitoring programs, close supervision and feedback are among the many strategies discussed. Teaching students with ADHD can be a challenge and teachers also need to monitor their own stress and frustration levels.

Chapter 4

Strategies to Help
Students Who are Inattentive,
but *Not* Hyperactive or Impulsive

While there has been a great deal of information written about children with ADHD who are hyperactive, impulsive, and inattentive (the combined type), there has been relatively little written about children with the predominantly inattentive type of ADHD.

These students call little attention to themselves. They are not disruptive. They generally do not annoy others. In fact, they may be quiet, shy, or even withdrawn. They tend to have problems with paying attention, organizing, and completing work.. They are often on the periphery of social relationships — not necessarily rejected by peers, but ignored.

Because they are usually quiet and often passive, children with the inattentive type of ADHD may not be diagnosed with a problem until they are older. Sometimes they can make it through much of school without major difficulty. When the work gets too hard for them to manage they begin to fall behind. They have trouble sustaining attention long enough to complete classwork and homework. They "tune out" and miss vital information in class. They may work slower than others and they often have a hard time starting tasks and organizing their time and materials. A student with the predominantly inattentive type of ADHD will exhibit many of the characteristics listed below:

    a.   often does not pay close attention to details

    b.   often makes careless mistakes in schoolwork, work, or other activities

    c.   often does not seem to listen when spoken to directly

    d.   often does not follow through on instructions and fails to complete schoolwork or other tasks

    e.   often has difficulty organizing tasks and activities

f.   often avoids and dislikes tasks that require concentration and a great deal of mental effort

g.   often loses things necessary for tasks or activities (e.g., toys, school assignments, pencils, books, or tools)

h.   is often easily distracted by extraneous stimuli

i.   is often forgetful in daily activities

Teaching Strategies to Help the Inattentive Student

• Question the student privately and try to determine why he is inattentive.

• Check to see if the work is too difficult for the student to understand or too easy and causing the student to be bored.

• The teacher should be aware of the sensitive nature of these students. Avoid criticism, especially public criticism which could embarrass the student. Speak to the student privately to address academic performance problems.

• Change your teaching style frequently during the day. Be animated, lively, dramatic, and enthusiastic. Your enthusiasm could capture the student's attention. Make lessons interesting, novel, and fun.

• Project your voice and vary the tone and inflection.

• Make direct eye contact to hold the student's attention and address the student by name periodically to focus attention.

• Problem solve with the student to find solutions to incomplete work and/or inattention. Perhaps the teacher and student can agree on strategies such as: a private signal by the teacher to remind the student to pay attention; breaking long seatwork assignments into smaller assignments; setting short-term goals; and seating the student in close proximity to the teacher.

- If the student is slow in processing and cannot complete work in a timely way, reduce the number of questions or problems assigned.

- Do not penalize student for poor handwriting. If handwriting is a problem and does not improve even with repetition make allowances. Reduce the amount of written work, do not grade on the basis of penmanship, etc.

- For students who are slow in copying homework assignments from the chalkboard try the following accommodations:
  a. post assignments on the Internet
  b. allow additional time to write homework
  c. pass out pre-written sheets containing homework assignment

- Forgetfulness and misplacing or losing things necessary for tasks is common for students with this type of ADHD. Encourage the student to use a checklist at the end of the school day to make sure all necessary materials are brought home. Parents can make a similar checklist at home to make sure all materials are returned to school the next day.

- Give the student a marble to keep in her pocket as a reminder (i.e., to bring a note back to school, do a specific assignment, etc.).

- Stick a Post-It® note on the cover of the student's book as a reminder. Encourage the student to keep a supply of Post-It® notes nearby for reminders.

- Insist that the student clean and organize his backpack, desk area, and notebooks at least once a week. Provide help when necessary.

- If reading, spelling, written language, or math skills are weak, refer the student for an evaluation to determine if there is evidence of a specific learning disability. Students with the inattentive type of ADHD tend to have a higher risk for learning problems.

- Implement a "point-of-performance" behavior management program to motivate the student to attend and complete work. Offer points or other rewards for completed work.

- Use an auditory self-monitoring system such as the *Listen, Look and Think Program* (Parker, 1991). The student listens to a special endless-cassette audio tape which emits a beep tone at different intervals. When the student hears the beep he is reminded to pay attention to his work. The student marks whether he was paying attention on a separate self-evaluation form when the tape beeps. Research has shown this to be an effective method to improve on-task behavior in class and when students do homework. The *Listen, Look and Think Program* is available through the A.D.D. WareHouse.

- Tape an index card on the student's desk. Divide the card in half with a marker. On the top left side of the card put a plus sign or "happy face" and on the top right side put a minus sign or "sad face." Record some soft music with gaps of no music. Play the tape and have the student mark on the "happy face" side of the card if he was on-task when the music started. Mark the "sad face" side if he was not on task when the music started. This can be done as a group or individually with headphones.

- Use the *Attention Training System* (ATS) developed by Dr. Michael Gordon to encourage the student to stay on task. The ATS automatically gives the student a point for every minute the student is on task. If the teacher notices the student off-task she presses a button on her remote unit and a point is deducted from the module on the student's desk. The ATS is available through the A.D.D. WareHouse or Gordon Systems Inc.

- Write a contract between you and the student in which the student agrees to do a certain amount of work.

- Find ways to make lessons interesting to the student.

- Avoid assignments that are dull and repetitive. Such assignments may take minutes for other students, but may take hours for the inattentive student to complete.

- Use a self-monitoring program such as *Pay Attention! Stop, Think & Listen* by Linda Bowman (1996) which is briefly described below.

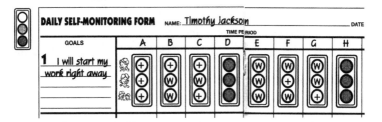

The student sets from one to four behavioral goals, i.e., starting work right way. The student and teacher each rate whether the student reached the goal during a specific time period. The student marks a "+" (reached goal) or "W" (did not reach goal) in the top row of the traffic light. The teacher marks the middle row. If the student accepts the teacher's rating without arguing he gets an extra "+" in the bottom row of the traffic light. The student could earn points which could be exchanged for rewards or privileges based on the total number of "+" marks earned.

• Communicate frequently with parents to keep them apprised of their child's progress. Be sensitive to possible problems at home with academics. Homework may need to be reduced if parents indicate that the child is spending excessive time trying to complete homework. Expectations for written work may need to be modified. Parents and teachers may need to join forces to help the inattentive student make friends and participate in social activities.

• Try these strategies to get the student's attention:
   ✓ Turn the room lights off and on.
   ✓ Say, "Everybody, listen up!"
   ✓ Use an overhead projector so you can face the students while presenting a lesson. Use colored markers to write on the overhead transparency. Color is a good way to grab a student's attention.
   ✓ Make eye contact during lesson presentation with the inattentive student.
   ✓ Grab the student's attention by acting silly, funny, or dramatic when presenting a lesson.

Summary

Inattentive students who do not show signs of hyperactivity or impulsivity may suffer from ADHD, predominantly inattentive type. These students are often very inattentive, off-task, and are described as "tuned out" or "in a world of their own." They can be shy, quiet, and slow in completing work. Socially they tend to be on the periphery of relationships with peers.

Chapter 5

Seven Principles for
Raising a Child with ADHD

This chapter is primarily for parents and will focus on how ADHD affects preschool children through adolescents. Raising a child or adolescent with ADHD requires parents to have a sound knowledge of ADHD, a good understanding, of behavior management, and the courage and persistence to actively support and advocate for their child.

The Preschool Child with ADHD

It is customary for preschool age children to be overactive and impulsive from time to time. Their attention is captured by things that interest them, but usually for short periods of time. They shift quickly from one activity to another. We expect preschoolers to be somewhat demanding, impulsive, or self-centered and generally we don't get too upset when they get frustrated and have occasional temper tantrums or crying spells. Hopefully we anticipate their frustration, plan for their short attention span, and vary their activities enough to sustain their interests.

Preschoolers with ADHD as *very* overactive and demanding. They are constantly moving, climbing,, and getting into things. They require constant supervision. Their high activity level, drivenness, and insatiable appetite for stimulation requires an ever watchful eye. They are often moody, irritable, and have temper outbursts when things don't go their way. Hitting and biting others is not an uncommon reaction to frustration.

At what point does activity exceed the bounds of normalcy and become hyperactivity? When is inattentiveness considered attention deficit? At what age should we expect immaturity end and impulsivity to disappear? Unfortunately there are no objective answers to these questions. We have no measures that differentiate between what is normal toddler behavior and "terrible 2's" behavior.

Parents of ADHD preschoolers often describe themselves as exhausted by the child rearing process. The typical methods of discipline such as time-out, positive reinforcement, and punishment don't work as well. They may try to discipline their youngsters and teach appropriate behavior, but the child seems unable to learn. Parents are often left without an effective means of control. Teachers of ADHD preschoolers end up equally frustrated. Disruptive behavior, especially aggression towards other children, becomes a chief concern for the teacher.

In preschoolers with severe hyperactivity, behavior modification does not work well. Behavior management is hampered by the child's lack of internal controls which are necessary to contain themselves even with the promise of immediate rewards or the threat of punishments. Parents of the more seriously involved kids are frequently asked to withdraw their child from the preschool only to end up in a desperate search for another school that will be able to handle their child's problems. Such places are rare, and often the parent ends up relying on the good graces of another preschool director or teacher who is willing to give their child a second (or third) chance.

Fortunately, the majority of the preschool age children described by their parents as inattentive and overactive will show improvement in these areas as they mature. However, for those children whose hyperactivity and conduct problems persist for at least one year, there is a much stronger likelihood that they will have continuing difficulty in these areas and may more likely receive a diagnosis of ADHD or oppositional defiant disorder in the future.

The Elementary School-Aged Child with ADHD

Most children with ADHD will be identified by the time they are nine or ten years of age.

If the child is primarily inattentive, but not necessarily hyperactive, he will leave a trail of unfinished tasks: uncovered toothpaste in the bathroom, clothes scattered about the floor of the bedroom, bed unmade, toys and books left wherever they were last used, games started and unfinished, tomorrow's math homework paper mixed in with last month's spelling, dresser drawers bulging from unfolded clothes, and on and on.

If hyperactivity and impulsivity are also present the picture at home becomes even more chaotic: toys scattered and broken, walls marked up, frequent family arguments over listening, meals disrupted by fighting, shopping trips marred by relentless demands, sibling conflicts, and frayed nerves.

Patterns of academic frustration and failure, social rejection, and criticism from parents and teachers build in elementary school to the point where other disorders associated with ADHD begin to appear. Approximately 60 percent of these children will develop oppositional disorder, characterized by defiant and non-compliant behavior. Frustrated by their lack of success, these children may become irritable and sullen. About half of this group of oppositional children will develop an even more serious behavior disorder in adolescence, namely conduct disorder (CD). Many ADHD children will suffer low self-esteem due to their inability to achieve the same levels of success as their peers. Still others will develop serious depression.

The Adolescent with ADHD

As many as 80 percent of children diagnosed with ADHD in early childhood will continue to have symptoms of overactivity, inattention, and impulsivity through adolescence.

As the child matures, ADHD symptoms may change qualitatively. The most striking difference is in motor activity. Hyperactivity, often so apparent in the young ADHD child, lessens by adolescence to the point where the teenager with ADHD may be indistinguishable from normal teens in that respect. Dr. Gabrielle Weiss and colleagues followed a large number of children with ADHD over time. When they were seen in adolescence at nearly 14 years of age, most of them still had symptoms of ADHD. Though they were better than when they were younger, they still showed impulsive cognitive styles, difficulties with attention, and were having significant academic problems as well. Low self-esteem, poor peer relationships, depressive symptoms, and problems with anti-social behavior can also be characteristic of adolescents with ADHD.

School problems can intensify in middle and high school. Greater demands are placed on students in secondary schools. They have more teachers to cope with, more work to be responsible for, more activities to organize, and they tend to be less closely supervised by teachers and parents. The ADHD adolescent starts middle school with several teachers each of whom probably has two hundred or more students to teach. It is easy to get lost in the shuffle.

Seven Principles for Parents of Children and Teens with ADHD

The following seven principles of parenting can guide you in parenting your ADHD child or adolescent.

Principle # 1: Provide unconditional love and positive regard.

Obviously, one of the most important things a parent can give their child is unconditional love. Nobody else has the capacity to feel towards your child as you do. Nobody else will care about your child as much as you do. And nobody else's love and caring mean as much to your child as yours does.

Life for kids with ADHD can be tough. Because of their difficulties in school they face failure and criticism every day from teachers who may not understand them and who are as frustrated with their behavior as parents are sometimes. They have a harder time making and keeping friends. They often get similar negative reactions from family members who may become worn out and frustrated.

We know that all this negative feedback has an effect on children with ADHD. Their rate of depression and low self-esteem is much greater. In a longitudinal study of ADHD children followed from early childhood to adulthood, investigators asked the grown subjects what made the most positive difference for them in their lives. Their response—having someone in their life that cared for them and had faith in them. Most likely this person would be a charsimatic adult such as a parent, although it could be another relative, a teacher, a friend or a neighbor.

"Having someone that cared about me!" That was the most important thing. Not medicine. Not counseling. Not grades in school.

Loving your child unconditionally means you love him for who he is, not for what he does. You show this unconditional love in your smile, your touch, your looks of concern, your interest, and by giving your time and attention. Your child will sense this and it may very well give him the strength he needs to face his world each and every day.

Consider the following suggestions when you communicate with your son or daughter.

- Listen to your child. Give your child your undivided attention when she has something to say.
- Avoid judging or criticizing. Children need understanding and guidance. When criticism is necessary, provide it in a constructive way.
- Be courteous and respectful when communicating.
- Express your affection and concern frequently. Tell your child you love her.
- Encourage your child to contribute their thoughts and ideas on issues.
- Look for positive accomplishments and offer praise.

Principle # 2: Spend enjoyable time with your child.

Child development experts believe giving time to your child impacts his development. Spending time and developing a close emotional bond shows your child you care.

Establishing a close relationship with your child can be a very rewarding experiences both for yourself and your child. You will be able to share your child's excitement, joy, fear, and frustration as he faces new challenges and experiences new adventures. It is thrilling and parents should try to be involved as much as possible.

Although as they get older, many children naturally try to distance themselves from their mothers and fathers, parents can do things to close the gap. Try to have some positive time together each week. Find an activity you both enjoy and do it together. Make this special time part of your weekly schedule. One father and son I know went to watch a movie every Wednesday evening. Another mother and son watched their favorite shows on television together a few nights a week. Some parents and their children have mutual interests in sports, and they play sports together or go to sporting events together.

You can't get to know your son or daughter without getting to know their friends as well. Try to make your house open to their friends. Welcome them and make them feel comfortable in your home. Encourage your son or daughter to invite friends for barbecues, family outings, short trips, etc.

Spend as much time as you can talking with your child. By spending time together, you will learn more about what he thinks, feels, and wants.

Principle # 3:   Become an ADHD expert.

Parents need to learn as much about ADHD as they can. Having knowledge about ADHD, the effect it can have on your child's behavior, socialization, school performance, and home life, will enable you to make the right decisions to best help your son or daughter. Fortunately, a great deal of information about ADHD exists. Books are readily available in national chain stores, through catalogs, and in schools and libraries. Many school districts offer parenting information and programs about ADHD. You can encourage your son or daughter to learn about ADHD as well. Books, videos, and newsletters have been published for children of all ages.

Learn about the resources available in your community that provide services to children with ADHD. You will need to know who the ADHD experts are in your area. Knowledge about treating children and adolescents with ADHD can vary widely among the educational and health care professionals in your community. Find out which ones know the most and have the most experience working with ADHD kids.

Get involved in your child's school. It is frequently at the start of middle school when many children with ADHD begin to have a great deal of trouble in school. As a parent you may have worked closely with your child's elementary school teachers. Maintain this close contact when your child transfers to a secondary school. With more teachers, more classes per day, more assignments to keep track of, and less personal attention given to students with special needs in middle and high school, your help may be needed if your child starts having trouble. Learn about your child's educational rights. Many students with ADHD will require some special assistance, either in a special education program or by having accommodations provided to him or her in regular education. If your student is having trouble in school, you will need to understand the public school's responsibility to assure that students receive the help they need.

Principle # 4: Model good values.

We must continue to teach our children good values—respect for others, respect for themselves, honesty, responsibility, morality, etc. These high principles in life are important. These principles are taught in school and preached in religious services, but must also be modeled by parents if they are to be incorporated in your child's value system.

Setting a good example for our children by showing them honesty, responsibility, and caring for others will be lessons that they can carry for their entire lives. Children with ADHD aren't generally dishonest, irresponsible, or uncaring. Lying, avoiding responsibility, hurtfulness towards others — those are not on the symptom list for ADHD. But, they are remarkably close to the list of characteristics found in children and teenagers who are diagnosed with social maladjustment and conduct disorder. These are the children who often come to the attention of the juvenile justice system, who are suspended or expelled from school, and who frequently have serious problems with substance abuse. Interesting, but not surprising, the best predictor of whether a child will develop conduct disorder is the presence of conduct disorder or anti-social behavior in his parents.

ADHD children and teenagers without conduct disorder typically don't have problems this severe. Although as a group they may not do as well educationally and career-wise as others without ADHD, they will generally turn out all right.

The message here is that one of the guiding principles in raising children with ADHD is to be a good example for them to follow. If your child doesn't keep his or her room organized, doesn't pay attention in class, or doesn't clean the car out once in a while — don't panic. In the long run these things may not be as important as the type of person he or she is becoming.

Principle # 5: Provide structure at home with clear, consistent rules.

Children with ADHD need structure — and lots of it. Structure means that parents should clearly spell out how they expect their child to act at home and away. We call these house rules and street rules. By having clear sets of rules for the child to live by parents set boundaries for behavior.

Many children can impose their own limits on their behavior. They have internalized a sense of what is right and wrong. They can control their behavior, and they behave appropriately. These kids seem to be born with a set of rules and the ability to follow them. ADHD kids are different. Their main problem is poor self-regulation. They have difficulty inhibiting behavior and that is what gets them in the most trouble. They get stimulated, become over-aroused, and out of control. "Managed by the moment" a parent of an ADHD child said. Everything else gets shut out.

We can surely provide our ADHD kids with rules about behavior. What we can't give them is the self-control they need to inhibit inappropriate behavior and follow the rules. We can make a rule that they can't use the phone until after their homework is done, but we can't give them the strength to restrain themselves from using the phone and the persistence to concentrate on their homework. Nevertheless, having rules are a good start and an important part of any program to manage behavior.

When your kids become teenagers, include them in the rule-making process. The "do it because I said so" approach isn't going to sit well with teens. They want to be heard and they have a right to express their opinion about issues that concern them. By using a democratic process to establish house rules, parents are less likely to make rules that are unrealistic for the adolescent to live by. Through discussion with parents in the rule-making process, teens are better able to see the reasoning behind certain restrictions and expectations. Furthermore, compliance with the rules will most likely be greater since the child had a say in constructing them.

Although it is usually better to use a democratic process in establishing house rules and street rules for teenagers, certain rules are going to be nonnegotiable. For instance: coming home on time, no smoking, no drinking alcohol, no using drugs; no violence or cursing; no staying out past curfew without asking permission; no skipping school; etc. Two sets of rules are useful—house rules and street rules.

Examples of common house rules are:
- Treat other members of the family with respect.
- Physical violence or foul language are not permissible any time.
- Family members are responsible for cleaning their own rooms.

- Eating is allowed only in the kitchen.
- No use of the telephone after 10:30 p.m.

Examples of common street rules are:
- The use of any alcohol or drugs is forbidden.
- You must arrive at school everyday by 7:30 a.m.
- Respect the property of others.
- Show courtesy to others.
- Obey the laws in the community.

Principle # 6: Monitor compliance with rules and check behavior regularly.

Behavior needs to be consistently monitored. Having a set of rules for your child to live by is worthless if you are not paying careful attention to whether anyone is following them. It is simply not good enough to wait until a violation of a rule comes to your attention. By then the violation may have gone on for so long that too much damage may have already been done.

For example, if your child has had a pattern of not completing homework, you might establish a rule that all homework given that day in school needs to be completed before going out, watching television, using the phone, etc. Once established as a rule, you can't assume that all is well if you don't hear any complaints from school about incomplete homework. If your child is known to have chronic problems with homework completion in the past, parents will have to monitor homework completion—whether they hear from the school or not. In fact, for children who may not be honest about disclosing homework assignments, closer communication with the school may be needed to make sure the student is being truthful. After the child has shown consistent improvement in this area over time, less supervision may be appropriate.

Children, and especially, teenagers, will balk over such close monitoring and parents may begin to think that nightly conflicts are just not worth the effort. "If he fails he fails!" some exhausted parents will say. But parents shouldn't fall prey to that kind of discouraged thinking. The rule should stand. Frequent monitoring should continue. When the teenager has demonstrated responsible behavior by completing homework, the parent can slowly back off.

Monitor your child's behavior, particularly in the teenage years. Check on her whereabouts, what she is doing, when she plans to be at a certain place, what time she will be home, what her friends are like, what her homework is, etc. This is part of the responsibility of being a parent. Teenagers, especially those with ADHD, require this kind of monitoring. Having someone in authority keep an eye on her behavior may reduce impulsivity and may make her think about consequences a little more. Most importantly, it sends a powerful message—you care enough about her to be concerned.

Principle # 7: Inspire confidence as a parent-coach.

Parents who act as coaches rather than critics will be able to provide more effective guidance to their child. It is natural to become defensive and defiant if criticized or judged. Children and adolescents with ADHD receive a great deal of criticism. This can lead to feelings of frustration, irritability, resentment, and self-doubt. For this reason, home should be a respite from life's daily pressures. This is especially true if your son's or daughter's problems stem from behavior which cannot be easily regulated. If you notice your child's problems are mounting, try to be a coach rather than a critic. Consider the following points.

- In general, all kids (and especially those with ADHD) do better when their environment has a lot of structure— frequent monitoring of behavior and feedback.

- . Feedback about behavior is most effective when it is <u>positive</u> and <u>encouraging</u>. Negative feedback, when it must be given, should be communicated without blame or derision. Parents shouldn't emphasize the negative as a first reaction. They should practice positive coaching techniques by giving as much positive reinforcement as possible.

- While negative consequences for inappropriate behavior are important to discourage the behavior from repeating, the parent-coach seizes every opportunity to build their child's confidence, solidify the parent-child relationship, and motivate their child to stay on track in the future.

Summary

The job of parents is to guide their child so he will acquire the skills needed to one day live independently and responsibly. For the child to learn these skills, parents must gradually loosen their control and let their child experience life for himself. Fortunately, most children find their way without running into too much difficulty. Children with ADHD, however, are at greater risk for behaving in ways that can have serious health consequences. They may also experience more difficulty in school, have more automobile crashes, get more traffic citations, and may develop substance abuse problems. Parents living with an ADHD child should be guided by several principles, which may improve the likelihood of positive outcomes and, hopefully, reduce future risks.

Chapter 6

Strategies to Help Students with ADHD and Other Psychological Disorders

A significant number of children with ADHD have other psychological disorders. Some exhibit oppositional behavior or more serious problems with conduct. Some suffer from anxiety and depression. Others may develop obsessive compulsive disorder, Tourette's syndrome, or motor tics. Many have significant social problems causing them to have few or no friends.

Students with psychological disorders often have certain patterns of behavior which occur over a prolonged period of time.

✓ difficulty making and keeping friends
✓ withdrawal from social activities
✓ somatic complaints (stomachaches, headaches, etc.)
✓ excessive lateness or absence from school
✓ statements or actions indicating lack of confidence or low self-esteem
✓ avoidance of difficult tasks
✓ feelings of sadness, discouragement, or hopelessness
✓ excessive worry
✓ irritability
✓ poor concentration due to worry or preoccupation
✓ lack of interest in school work
✓ easily frustrated
✓ aggressiveness
✓ defiance

Symptoms of a psychological disorder can reach a level where there is significant impairment in a child's functioning at home, school, or in the community or work setting. Make a referral for an evaluation to better understand the nature, causes, and the

69

severity of the student's problem. Below are descriptions of different psychological disorders which can co-occur with ADHD.

Oppositional Defiant Disorder and Conduct Disorder

Up to 40 percent of children and as many as 65 percent of adolescents with ADHD exhibit such degrees of stubbornness and noncompliance they fall into a category of disruptive behavior disorder known as *oppositional defiant disorder*. Below is a list of characteristics of oppositional defiant disorder.

1. often loses temper
2. often argues with adults
3. often actively defies or refuses to comply with adults' requests or rules
4. often deliberately annoys people
5. often blames others for his or her mistakes or misbehavior
6. is often touchy or easily annoyed by others
7. is often angry and resentful
8. is often spiteful or vindictive

Conduct disorder co-occurs with ADHD in about 30 percent of children and adolescents referred for treatment. Adolescents with conduct disorder may exhibit behavior which is characterized by aggression to people and animals, destruction of property, deceitfulness or theft, and serious violation of rules. Below is a list of characteristics of conduct disorder.

Aggression to people and animals

1. often bullies, threatens, or intimidates others
2. often initiates physical fights
3. has used a weapon that can cause serious physical harm to others (e.g., a bat, brick, broken bottle, knife, gun)
4. has been physically cruel to people
5. has been physically cruel to animals
6. has stolen while confronting a victim (e.g., mugging, purse snatching, extortion, armed robbery

7. has forced someone into sexual activity

Destruction of property

8. has deliberately engaged in fire setting with the intention of causing serious damage
9. has deliberately destroyed others' property (other than by fire setting)

Deceitfulness or theft

10. has broken into someone else's house, building, or car
11. often lies to obtain goods or favors or to avoid obligations (i.e., "cons" others)
12. has stolen items of nontrivial value without confronting a victim (e.g., shoplifting, but without breaking and entering; forgery)

Serious violations of rules

13. often stays out at night despite parental prohibition, beginning before age 13 years
14. has run away from home overnight at least twice while living in parental or parental surrogate home (or once without returning for a lengthy period)
15. often truant from school, beginning before age 13 years

The severity of conduct disorder ranges from mild to severe based on the number of symptoms demonstrated and the degree of harm rendered to person or property. There are two broad groups of adolescents with conduct disorder. In one group are adolescents who had an early onset of symptoms of conduct disorder. Those in this group developed symptoms before age 10. They are more likely to have antisocial behavior problems throughout life. In the second group are adolescents who had a later onset of symptoms of conduct disorder. Those in this group developed symptoms after the age of 10. Their antisocial problems are not as chronic and persistent and are not likely to continue beyond adolescence.

As with oppositional defiant disorder, when ADHD and conduct disorder co-occur, problems can multiply. Early intervention is extremely important to prevent serious antisocial behavior, substance abuse, and potential delinquency. Parents will benefit from learning behavior management strategies. Treatment with medication can improve symptoms of aggression, defiance, and irritability as well as targeting ADHD symptoms. Educational interventions can reduce stress on the student and may make school a more positive experience.

Teachers can use the following strategies to help students with behavioral problems such as oppositional disorder or conduct disorder.

- Model appropriate social behavior. State commands and instructions in a respectful manner.

- Post clear rules of classroom behavior. Review these rules frequently. Point out positive instances where students followed these rules and offer praise and reward when indicated.

- Provide structure to students who are likely to act out. Closely monitor their behavior, especially during transitions or during stress times of the day.

- Use proximity control to project authority and to easily cue students to behave. Standing by the student with a stern look may encourage the student to obey.

- Prior to a new activity, review how you expect the students in your class to behave.

- Quickly intervene if a student's behavior or emotions are getting out of control. Move closer to the student, redirect the focus of attention, and remind the student to behave appropriately.

- Use "prudent" reprimands for misbehavior. A prudent reprimand is one which directs the student to stop inappropriate behavior without causing shame, embarrassment, or unnecessary attention. Imprudent reprimands contain unnecessary lectures, threats, belittling remarks, etc.

- Examine antecedents of a student's misbehavior to determine if factors in the environment may be precipitating the unwanted reactions.

- Seat student near quiet students who may have a positive impact.

- Use a nonverbal signal with the disruptive student (a look, gesture, etc.) to help the student realize his or her behavior needs to be modified.

- Use humor to defuse a potential problem situation.

- Keep student occupied with work or appropriate activities to prevent opportunities for acting out.

- Plan ahead and try to foresee potential problem situations.

- Increase the frequency and the immediacy of rewards and praise.

- For oppositional children, do not overreact to minor disruption. It may be more helpful to ignore a minor outburst than to confront the student, especially if confrontation generally leads to escalation of the behavior.

- Give the student who loses his or her temper some time to cool off. Give the student an opportunity to walk somewhere else in the room, run a quick errand, or get some water. This break can prevent an aggressive outburst and defuse an otherwise volatile situation.

- Have an intervention plan ready in case a student's behavior escalates out of control. Call for help from an administrator. Ask the student to leave the room and visit another teacher or a guidance counselor who could help the student quiet down. Try not to get into a power struggle with the student as this typically escalates negative situations.

- Use behavioral contracts, token programs, a home-school daily report card to set goals and provide the student with the opportunity to earn privileges for appropriate behavior. See earlier chapter on behavior problems for additional ideas.

Depression and Bipolar Disorder

Children and teens with ADHD may be at greater risk for developing depressive disorders. It is estimated that as many as 30 percent develop symptoms of depression.

One type of depression is known as *dysthymia*. Children and adolescents with dysthymia have low mood most of the day, more often than not, for at least one year. Their low mood may take the form of irritability. In addition, they may have symptoms of poor appetite or overeating, insomnia or hypersomnia, low energy, low self-esteem, poor concentration, and feelings of hopelessness.

Another type of depression children and adolescents may develop is known as *major depression*. Those with major depression have depressed mood most of the day nearly every day for at least two weeks. Other symptoms include: deriving little or no pleasure from activities; significant weight loss when not dieting or less weight gain than expected; insomnia or hypersomnia nearly every day; low energy; feelings of worthlessness or inappropriate guilt nearly every day; diminished ability to think, concentrate, or make decisions; and recurrent thoughts of death.

Children and adolescents with ADHD are also at greater risk to develop *bipolar disorder*. People with bipolar disorder have frequent and rapid dramatic shifts of mood including elation, depression, irritability, and anger. At times they may have an exaggerated positive view of themselves, believing they are right and others wrong. Their speech may become "pressured" marked by intense rapid talking and accompanied by "racing thoughts" they cannot control. In addition to the symptoms noted above, a family history of bipolar disorder, severe symptoms of ADHD, oppositional disorder, and conduct disorder are markers that could signal the presence of bipolar disorder.

Teachers can use the following strategies to help students who suffer from dysthymia or depression.

- Ease negative mood by complimenting positive behavior and bring the student's focus to positive things.

- Look for signs of stress and provide encouragement or reduced work load.

- Spend more time talking to students who seem pent up.

- Train anger control. Encourage student to walk away and use calming strategies.

- If the student seems unhappy with school, talks about dropping out, or seems unhappy in general try these additional strategies:
  ✓ emphasize student's strengths and abilities
  ✓ find ways the student can succeed
  ✓ praise in public; reprimand in private
  ✓ mark correct responses on tests/assignments, not errors
  ✓ prohibit any humiliation or teasing from other students
  ✓ arrange for meeting with parents and other teachers to find ways to help student feel better about school and/or self
  ✓ consider referral to child study team for help

Teachers can use the following strategies to help students with bipolar disorder.

- Some children with bipolar disorder may be easily distracted. Seat the student in a low-distraction area of the classroom.

- Have the student sit near the teacher.

- Bipolar students may have severe mood swings. The teacher should avoid arguing with the student. Set firm boundaries with appropriate consequences. Schedule frequent breaks to give the student a chance to relax. Use a private signal to alert the student if he needs to calm down.

- Give the student an extra minute or two to process instructions when asked to do something or to make a decision.

- If the student has difficulty with transitions allow her to finish a task before moving on to another one. Give warnings and prompts to the next task.

- Reassure and be supportive, especially if you sense the student is getting tense or anxious about something that is coming up. Allow the student to explain his feelings to you.

- Maintain a calm demeanor. Be flexible, emotionally sensitive to the student, and understanding.

Anxiety Disorders

Children and adolescents with ADHD are more likely to have anxiety related disorders. Two of the more common types of anxiety disorders that occur are *separation anxiety disorder* and *overanx-*

ious disorder. Below is a list of characteristics of children who suffer from separation anxiety disorder.

1. recurrent, excessive distress when separation from home or a major attachment figure (i.e., parent or other relative) occurs or is anticipated
2. persistent and excessive worry about losing, or about possible harm befalling, major attachment figures
3. persistent and excessive worry that an untoward event will lead to separation from a major attachment figure (e.g., getting lost or being kidnapped)
4. persistent reluctance or refusal to go to school or elsewhere because of fear of separation
5. persistently and excessively fearful or reluctant to be alone without major attachment figures at home or without significant adults in other settings
6. persistent reluctance or refusal to go to sleep without being near a major attachment figure or to sleep away from home
7. repeated nightmares involving the theme of separation
8. repeated complaints of physical symptoms (such as headaches, stomachaches, nausea, or vomiting) when separation from major attachment figures occurs or is anticipated

Overanxious disorder of childhood may exist if there is excessive anxiety and worry about a number of events or activities (such as school) occurring more days than not for at least six months. The child or adolescent with this type of anxiety disorder finds it difficult to control worrying and may have some of the following additional symptoms: restlessness or feeling keyed up or on edge; becoming easily fatigued; difficulty concentrating or their mind going blank; irritability; muscle tension; and a sleep disturbance that can cause difficulty falling asleep, staying asleep, or having a restful sleep.

Teachers can use the following strategies to help students with anxiety disorders.

- Provide reassurance and encouragement. Children suffering from anxiety or depression often have low self-esteem, they worry excessively, and often withdraw from others. A support relationship with a meaningful adult can make a very big difference to these children.

- Try to understand factors that may be causing the student to become upset. By helping the student sort out his or her feelings the teacher may help the child feel better.

- Speak softly in a non-threatening manner if student shows nervousness.

- Review instructions when giving new assignments to make sure student comprehends. If you notice a student is confused or nervous, provide additional attention to help her understand instructions and to reassure.

- Look for opportunities for student to display leadership role in class.

- Focus on student's talents and accomplishments. Psychologist, Dr. Robert Brooks, encourages teachers to find each child's special talent or "island of competence" and build on it.

- Conference frequently with parents to learn about student's interests and achievements.

- Assign student to be a peer teacher. Peer teaching can be a great help to students who need additional instruction to boost confidence.

- Make time to talk alone with student.

- Encourage social interactions with classmates if student is withdrawn or excessively shy.

- Reinforce frequently when signs of frustration are noticed.

Obsessive Compulsive Disorder (OCD)

Approximately 25 percent of people with *obsessive-compulsive disorder* (OCD) have ADHD. OCD is characterized by the following behavior patterns:

1. intrusive, forceful, and repetitive thoughts, images, or sounds that are lodged in one's mind and cannot be willfully eliminated
2. compulsions to perform motor or mental acts
3. excessive and recurrent doubting about matters of either major or minor importance

The obsessions or compulsions cause marked distress, are time consuming, and significantly interfere with normal functioning. Many children with OCD are secretive about their condition so it may be difficult for teachers to identify symptoms.

Examples of obsessive or compulsive behavior in children and adolescents may include: fear of contamination and overconcern with cleanliness; repeated hand washing; fear of harm, illness, or death; unusual or overly rigid eating habits; excessive concern about the tidyness of their room and their belongings; compulsion to place items around the house in a particular way; repeated checking if something is on or off, locked or unlocked; ritualistic counting; repetition of a series of acts before moving on to something else; obsessions revolving around a need for symmetry, fear of sharp objects, etc. Jack Nicholson did a wonderful job of portraying a person with OCD in the award-winning movie, *As Good As It Gets!*

To identify students with this disorder teachers must become knowledgeable about OCD. Treatment for OCD usually involves a combination of medication and cognitive-behavior therapy. When

ADHD is also present, the treatment can become much more complicated. Multiple medications may be prescribed to treat both disorders.

Teachers can use the following strategies to help students with OCD.

- Do not punish the student for situations or behaviors over which he has no control (i.e., the student may be tardy or absent because of adherence to rituals, the student may not be able to finish a writing assignment on time because of numerous cross-outs/erasures/checking, etc.).

- If the student with OCD has difficulty taking notes or writing due to writing compulsions, consider accommodations such as use of a tape recorder, a student scribe, or reduce amount of written work required.

- Do not allow other students to tease the child with OCD because of rituals or fears.

- Provide support and understanding to parents. Understand that the child's disorder can put a great deal of stress on the family.

- If the OCD student has reading compulsions the teacher may tape-record chapters in texts, allow others to read to the student, or assign shorter reading assignments.

- Allow accommodations for test-taking if the OCD student has difficulty taking tests. Allow extra time, provide a different location, permit the student to write directly on the test booklet rather than filling out computer test forms, allow the student to take the test orally.

- While most students with OCD try their best, some may try to use OCD as a crutch to avoid schoolwork or homework. If you suspect this is occurring coordinate your teaching strategies with the parents and with the child's counselor or therapist if one is available.

Asperger's Disorder

Asperger's Disorder is an impairment in social interaction, which was first described in the 1940s. Children and adolescents with Asperger's have impaired social interactions and unusual patterns of communication and behavior.

When communicating, they exhibit some of the following symptoms:

1. a marked impairment in nonverbal behaviors used to communicate with others such as eye contact, facial expression, body postures, and gestures
2. failure to develop friendships appropriate to one's age and development
3. failure to seek out others to communicate
4. lack of social reciprocity when interacting with others.

Those affected by Asperger's seem uninterested in social interaction. They have difficulty predicting other people's behavior, leading to a fear or avoidance of others. They may not understand the intentions of others or the motives behind other people's behavior. They often do not clearly understand their own emotions and have trouble explaining their behavior. They lack empathy.

Those with Asperger's also exhibit unusual behavior patterns including preoccupation with a specific interest; inflexible adherence to specific routines or rituals; repetitive motor mannerisms (such as hand or finger flapping or twisting or whole body movements); preoccupation with parts of objects.

Asperger's disorder is rare and is not frequently seen in those with ADHD. However, some people with Asperger's also have problems with hyperactivity, impulsivity, and inattention. For some, this may be caused by the Asperger's itself, while others may have a co-diagnosis of ADHD.

Teachers can use the following strategies to help students with Asperger's disorder.

- Be explicit when giving instructions. Don't assume that the student understands what you have said.

- Draw the child's attention to the use of gesture, facial expression, eye direction, and closeness of social interactions to convey meaning to what is being said.

- Help the student understand the meaning behind what others say.

- Explain "pretending" and help the student discriminate between pretend and reality.

- Explain the child's role in certain tasks, situations and event.

- Avoid ambiguity. Use a visual model when possible to clarify what you mean.

- Maintain a calm classroom environment with structure and clear rules.

- Understand the student's limited ability to interpret social cues. Help in teaching appropriate social interaction skills, such as taking turns, cooperating, sharing, etc.

- Guide other students to help them understand the social differences in the Asperger student.

- Support the student in physical activities if clumsiness is a problem.

- Simplify your communications with the student. Give one instruction at a time. Keep your facial expressions and gestures simple and clear. Give the child a chance to respond.

- Be aware that the student may prefer to be alone rather than in close contact with other students. Give the student time to get to know others. Move slowly, but positively in introducing new people.

Tics and Tourette's Syndrome

Tics are sudden, repetitive, and involuntary movements of muscles. Vocal tics involve muscles that control speech and cause involuntary sounds such as coughing, throat clearing, sniffing, making loud sounds, grunting, or calling out words. Motor tics involve other muscles and can occur in any part of the body. Some examples of motor tics are eye blinking, shoulder shrugging, facial grimacing, head jerking, and a variety of hand movements. Tics that are less common involve self-injurious behavior such as hitting or biting oneself and coprolalia (involuntary use of profane words or gestures). When these types of tics occur many times a day, nearly every day for at least four weeks, but for no longer than 12 consecutive months, the child may have a transient tic disorder.

It is estimated that 10 percent of children and adolescents with ADHD will develop a transient tic disorder. Others may develop a tic disorder that is associated with the use of stimulant medication.

A child who has either a motor or a vocal tic (but not both), which occurs many times a day, nearly every day, for a period of at least one year (without stopping for more than three months), may be diagnosed as having a chronic tic disorder. *Tourette's syndrome* is a chronic tic disorder characterized by both multiple motor tics and one or more vocal tics, although not necessarily concurrent. These tics are more severe than the simple, transient motor tics described earlier. They occur many times a day, nearly every day or intermittently throughout a period of more than one year. They involve the head and frequently other parts of the body such as the torso, arms, and legs. Vocal tics may include the production of sounds like clucking, grunting, yelping, barking, snorting, and coughing. Utterances of obscenities, coprolalia, are rare and occur in about 10 percent of children with Tourette's.

Dr. David Comings and Dr. Brenda Comings, of the City of Hope Medical Center in Duarte California, studied 130 patients with Tourette's. They found that more than half of them had ADHD. Stimulants should be used cautiously with children who have chronic tic disorder or Tourette's syndrome and ADHD.

Teachers can use the following strategies to help students with tic disorders or Tourette's syndrome.

• Ignore the tics. The teacher's reaction to the student's tics can make a critical difference in the student's life. Teachers should understand that tics are the result of a brain-based condition and are performed in response to insistent sensory urges (something like an itch). Do not express frustration, annoyance, or anger at the student for exhibiting a tic.

• Tics tend to worsen when the student is under stress. Students with Tourette's syndrome perform best when they are in a calm, supportive environment.

• Most children with tics or Tourette's are embarrassed and frustrated by their tics. Help the child develop strategies for coping with tics in the classroom.

• Help other children in the classroom be sensitive to the student with tics. Teach them to ignore the student's tics.

• Extend time limits on tests. Tics occur in bouts and these bouts can occur at inopportune times.

• The student may be able to suppress a tic for awhile and may need to leave the room for a short time to release or let out tics.

Other Characteristics of Children with Psychological Problems

Children with psychological problems often have trouble with making and keeping friends, arriving to class on time, absenteeism, and completing work in school.

Teachers can use the following strategies to help students who have social problems.

• If a student has few or no friends ask the student who he might like to work with in class and arrange for small group activities so the two students can interact.

• Praise the student in public to increase the positive perceptions of classmates.

• Consider referring the student to a social skills training group. See chapter on social skills training for more information.

• Make sure the student is included in games or activities during recess or breaks.

• Meet with parents to give them suggestions about other students in class who could be potential friends.

• If grooming or hygiene is a problem talk about it with the student or the parents.

• Model appropriate social behavior, praise and encourage appropriate social behavior in the student. Reinforce the student for being polite to others, sharing, and cooperating.

Teachers can use the following strategies to help students who are excessively late or absent.

• Praise the student for being on time or offer a reward for promptness (i.e., free time for an activity of the student's choice, homework pass for coming on time every day, etc.).

- Enlist the cooperation of the parent to help make sure the student leaves the house on time and has the means to be at school on time.

- Make a chart for the student to keep track of tardiness and absences so the student could see progress.

- Ask the student if there are specific obstacles to coming to school on time (i.e., problems with transportation, family issues, health issues, etc.).

- Ask a student who lives nearby if he or she could walk to school with the student to encourage on-time behavior.

- Encourage parents and student to get all school materials ready the night before to avoid any morning delays.

Teachers can use the following strategies to help students who do not complete work.
- Give clear instructions on how you want work done and when you expect it to be completed.

- Monitor student's classwork closely. Walk around the room and encourage student to attend to work. If the student shows signs of confusion, offer assistance and explain assignment if necessary.

- Assign a 'study buddy' to student to help keep the student on track with work effort.

- Give shorter assignments or allow student to complete a section of a longer assignment given to other classmates.

- If handwriting is difficult for the student, compensate by allowing word processor, oral answers, or minimize large amounts of handwriting in assignments.

- Provide praise and reward for student when work is completed and turned in on time.

- Break the assignment down into smaller parts for student and set time limit for each part. At the end of each time period monitor the student's progress and provide structure and feedback as necessary.

- Praise other students seated around the student to encourage proper work habits.

- Stay in close proximity to student during independent seat work.

Summary

Students with ADHD often have other psychological disorders which can affect their behavior and academic performance. If you notice the student has difficulty making and keeping friends, is withdrawn, has frequent somatic complaints, is excessively late or absent from school, has low self-esteem, worries excessively, appears sad and depressed, or is irritable, aggressive and defiant the student may have another psychological disorder that should be considered.

Refer the student to guidance or to the child study team for an evaluation. Teachers can help students with other psychological disorders by providing understanding and using specific classroom strategies to help the student adjust.

Chapter 7

Teaching Study Strategies

Organizational Strategies

Students who organize their materials, their time, and their school assignments often do well in school. Unfortunately, a common characteristic of students with ADHD is chronic disorganization. As one fifteen year old recently said, "I start off the year great. New notebook, clean backpack, all new pens and pencils, but by the end of the second week it's all a mess and I can never get it back together."

Disorganization is often cited by teachers as the biggest problem their students face. It pays to spend time each day reminding students how to get themselves organized so they can develop good organization habits. Consider the strategies below.

- Encourage students to use the following strategies to stay organized:
  - use a homework assignment book
  - write down all assignments when they are given
  - Prioritize assignments
  - use a calendar to keep track of long term projects, appointments, tests, and due dates of assignments
  - sort through desk and locker at school to maintain neatness
  - refer to assignment book and calendar often

- Draw a diagram of the inside of the student's desk and/or locker indicating exact placement of books and materials. Tape the diagram to the inside so student can refer to it as often as necessary.

- Pass out a list of school supplies you expect your students to have on hand either in class or at home for homework. These items may be included on the list:

• 3-ring notebook	• spiral notebooks
• dividers with pockets	• pen/pencil holder
• assignment planbook	• appointment book
• calendar to schedule work	• electronic organizer
• dictionary	• thesaurus
• atlas	• encyclopedia
• Internet access	• index cards and box
• folders to store papers	• writing tools
• pencil sharpener	• ruler, compass, protractor
• markers and highlighters	• glue stick, tape
• scissors, hole punch	• stapler and staples
• paper clips	• rubber bands
• Post-It® notes	• reinforcers for notebook
• "accordion" files	• clear plastic bins
• bulletin board and colored stick pins	• stopwatch or timer

- Many students have trouble managing time. For students with ADHD time management seems impossible. Students with the inattentive type of ADHD may have difficulty getting started on tasks. They procrastinate and often need frequent prompts to get them going. The hyperactive-impulsive ADHD students have trouble stopping enjoyable tasks and starting ones that are less attractive. They both have difficulty planning how to spend their time. Teach time management strategies such as: daily, weekly, monthly planning; prioritizing, using "Do Lists."

- Weekly planning. Have the student make a weekly planner to map out time commitments for the week. This could include class time, time set aside for homework and studying, work time, or time for recreation and appointments.

- Monthly planning can be done using a calendar with daily squares large enough to write notes. Students could keep track of assignments, study times, appointments, after school activities, long term projects, etc.

- Explain how much time is wasted each day by people waiting for something to happen and how we could make better use of time. Suggest that students carry a book, class notes, make calls, or catch up on assignments while waiting.

- Teach lessons on how to overcome procrastination. Ask students to give examples of times they have procrastinated and elicit solutions from students about times they have overcome procrastination.

- Help students prepare "Do Lists" to prioritize their work. When something is written on the list the student gives it a number from 1 to 3 to indicate the priority. Items on the list marked "1" should be done first.

Note-taking Strategies

Taking good notes in class or from material read from a textbook or other sources can be important for successful learning. Note-taking becomes more important as students proceed through middle school and high school. Note-taking provides a means by which students can maintain and organize information. Good information management will be a big advantage to students when they are preparing for class, studying for exams, or writing research papers.

    Study Strategies Made Easy (Davis, et al.,1996) describes several types of notes and skills students should learn about to be effective note-takers.

- simple outlining
- mind mapping
- combo notes

- using abbreviations
- using recall questions to study
- improving listening skills
- taking notes from lectures
- adding textbook notes to lecture notes

Simple Outlining

Outlining provides a way for students to organize information in notes and a means by which to identify the main ideas and supporting details of lectures or reading selections. Students should be taught how to construct an outline.

- When outlining a reading selection such as a book chapter, the section or chapter title will be the title of the outline.
- Roman numerals designate the headings or topics of a chapter.
- Capital letters designate the subheadings or subtopics of a chapter.
- Arabic numerals designate supporting details.
- Lower case letters designate subdetails within supporting details.

Below is a sample outline:

```
                    Title
            I. Heading/Topic
               A. Main idea
                  1. Supporting detail
                  2. Supporting detail
                     a. Subdetail
                     b. Subdetail
               B. Main idea
                  1. Supporting detail
                  2. Supporting detail
                     a. Subdetail
                     b. Subdetail
```

Mind Mapping

Mind mapping is another strategy students can use to organize and manage information acquired through lectures or reading selections. Mind maps are less formal than simple outlines and allow the student to create their own pattern by which to organize information. Davis, et al. point out several steps students should use in making a mind map.

1. Identify the main ideas and supporting details of a reading selection.
2. Write the subject or topic in the center of the page and draw a box or circle around it.
3. Write the main ideas that have to do with the topic.
4. Connect a line from the topic to each main idea and list the main ideas.
5. List all details that connect to the main ideas they support.

SIZE   STRUCTURE

human brain 1/50th   Cerebrum Cerebellum   Medulla Oblongata
size of body
elephant brain 1/1000

HOW DOES THE BRAIN CONTROL BEHAVIOR?

FUNCTION   OTHER FACTS

Cerebrum Cerebellum Medulla   Each region has purpose
5 senses   movement   respiration   brains gets smaller with age
sight   balance   heart rate   improve mem. by exercise
sound   coordination   medicines may improve
taste   neurotransmitters affect beh.
touch
smell

Combo Notes

Combo notes is a method of organizing information which combines simple outlining and mind mapping. Instead of using roman numerals and letters, the student might use circles, boxes, stars, and other signs to designate main ideas, supporting details, and subdetails.

Using Abbreviations

Notetaking is made faster and easier by using common abbreviations such as ones listed below:

Symbols		*A Few Letters Only*	
#	number	amt	amount
%	percent	assoc	association, associate
$	money, dollars	b/c	because
+	plus, and, more	bio	biology, biography
-	negative, not, no	cont	continue(d)
=	equal	def	definition
≠	unequal, does not equal	eg, ex	for example
>	greater than	etc.	et cetera, also, so forth
<	less than	govt	government
≥	equal to or greater than	info	information
≤	equal to or less than	intro	introduce, introduction
re	regarding, about	pp	pages
\	therefore	s/t	something, sometimes
±	about, more or less	w/	with
@	at, per, each	w/o	without

Note: from Leslie Davis, Sandi Sirotowitz, and Harvey C. Parker (1996). Study Strategies Made Easy. Florida: Specialty Press, Inc. Copyright 1996 by Leslie Davis and Sandi Sirotowitz. Reprinted with permission

- use key words, not complete sentences
- omit unimportant words such as: "a," "the," "to," etc.
- develop their own system of abbreviating

Using Recall Questions

By using recall questions a student can turn notes into study sheets. Recall questions ask who, what, where, when, why, and how and should be written in the margins of notes. They can be valuable aids in studying and can help the student remember factual information.

Listening Strategies

Good note taking requires good listening skills. Listening in class can often be improved by providing the textbook chapter the night before the lecture so the student has an idea of what to listen for and what to write down. Taking notes will also help students focus on the lecture. In this way, students become active participants instead of passive observers. Students should also pay attention to the lecturer's verbal, presentation and body language cues to determine if a piece of information is important.

Some General Rules for Note-taking

• Instruct students to keep notes well organized. All notes for a particular class should be maintained in a spiral notebook or section of a looseleaf binder dedicated to that class only.

• Notes should be further organized by main topics and supporting ideas and details.

• Write only information that is important in notes.

• Instruct students to highlight or underline any new vocabulary words or terms.

• Emphasize that students should review notes as soon after class as possible. Fill in any gaps and look over notes each day and again before the next class session.

- If the student has poor note taking skills consider these strategies:
  - review instructions on how to outline or mind map, allow use of a note taker
  - instruct how to make an outline or mind-mapping
  - teacher supplies copy of notes
  - portable computers
  - supply copy of another student's notes
  - allow use of a tape recorder

Memory Strategies

Learning requires both understanding and memory. Without either it is impossible to fully benefit from education. There are essentially three types of memory: immediate memory, short-term memory, and long-term memory. Immediate memory enables us to recall information we were recently exposed to (i.e., when a telephone number is given to you). Short-term memory enables us to briefly retain information from a few hours or a few days. Long-term memory enables us to retain information for weeks, months, or years. There are strategies students can use to improve the storage of information into memory. In their book, *Study Strategies Made Easy*, Davis, et al. (1996) describe nine different memory techniques to improve recall: acrostics, acronyms, charting, visual emphasis, visualization, association, word linking, story linking, and rehearsal. These techniques can be taught in school.

- Acrostics. Teach the student to use mnemonics to improve recall. A mnemonic is a trick that helps you remember something. For example, the mnemonic to remember the planets is order is: My Very Educated Mother Just Served Us Nine Pickles—Mercury, Venus, Earth, Mars, Jupiter, Saturn, Uranus, Neptune, and Pluto.

- Acronyms. An acronym is a short version of an acrostic. An acronym uses the first letter of each concept to be learned to form one word. For example, to remember the Great Lakes—**H**uron, **O**ntario, **M**ichigan, **E**rie, Superior—**HOMES**.

- Encourage students to use visualization to improve re-call. By visualizing (forming mental pictures) of facts or concepts we can strengthen our recall. For example, to remember a new vocabulary word try to form a picture in your mind that conveys the meaning.

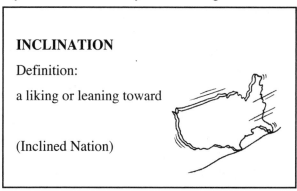

INCLINATION

Definition:

a liking or leaning toward

(Inclined Nation)

- Teach students how to form associations between facts or concepts to improve recall. For example, Davis, et al. (1996) give the example of a student using visualization to help remember that BRUSSELS is the capital of BEL-GIUM. To do this you can associate the word BRUS-SELS to brussel spouts and BELGIUM to Belgium waffles.

Note: from Leslie Davis, Sandi Sirotowitz, and Harvey C. Parker (1996). Study Strategies Made Easy. Florida: Specialty Press, Inc. Copyright 1996 by Leslie Davis and Sandi Sirotowitz. Reprinted with permission

Steps in Writing a Research Paper

1. Select an appropriate topic. Help the student understand that choosing a topic that is too broad or too narrow could make it difficult to write about.
2. Do preliminary research to find out if there is enough information about the topic to fulfill the assignment.
3. Collect sources such as encyclopedias, on-line sources, books, periodicals, etc.
4. Narrow the topic to your specific area of interest.
5. Write a thesis statement—a sentence that states the central theme of the paper.
6. List the main ideas that should be included in the paper and organize the sequence in which they will be included in the paper.
7. List details for each of the main ideas and put in outline form and on note cards.
8. Put the main ideas and details in sentence form in a rough draft.
9. Check spelling, capitalization, and punctuation.
10. Have someone proofread the rough draft.
11. Make certain the rough draft proves the point of the paper and backs it up with facts in a logical order.
12. Rewrite the paper in final form and ask someone to proofread once again.
13. Prepare final copy.

Test-taking Strategies

Students in all grades take tests and could benefit from learning strategies that may improve their test performance.

- The most common mistake students make when taking tests is they don't read instructions carefully. Show students how they can benefit by underlining key words in instructions and by taking their time to fully understand what they are supposed to do before they proceed.

- Encourage students to take an inventory of the study strategies they use to prepare for tests. Does the student:
  - ✓ start studying well in advance of the test
  - ✓ look over the chapter each night
  - ✓ read the class notes each night
  - ✓ use recall questions to review for a test
  - ✓ have someone quiz them to see how well the information is learned
  - ✓ make notes of the study material that is to be best remembered
  - ✓ read the content over and over
  - ✓ wait until the last minute to study and then cram
  - ✓ get very nervous before a test and can they relax
  - ✓ look over previous tests the teacher has given to get some idea of the types of questions that may be asked next time
  - ✓ review how they answered questions on previous tests to get some idea of what types of answers the teacher may be looking for
  - ✓ save old tests
  - ✓ write answers to possible essay questions in advance
  - ✓ use a highlighter to highlight important information in books or class notes
  - ✓ study with other students in a small group

Summary

Students of all ages can benefit from learning study strategies. Study strategies can greatly enhance a student's ability to stay organized, manage time, take notes in class from lectures and from books, listen attentively, memorize and recall information, write papers, and prepare for tests. Teaching study strategies should be part of the curriculum at every grade level. Students with ADHD, in particular, could benefit from strategies aimed at improving organizational skills, planning, and time management. All of the strategies in this chapter are considered by teachers to be essential for school success.

Chapter 8

Teaching Social Skills

Jody is a nine-year-old fourth grader. She is extremely timid. Her parents feel she is missing out socially because of her shyness. Her teachers would tell her parents she was the perfect student, but too quiet. Jody rarely speaks to other children and stays to herself most of the time.

David is anything but quiet. He is loud and boisterous and can get on your nerves if you're with him for more than 10 minutes. He never seems to notice when others are irritated with him. His parents say he was born with a megaphone in his mouth. They often go to another room when David is home just to get some peace and quiet. David usually finds them and keeps right on talking. His parents hoped that when he got into high school he'd become more aware of his behavior and would quiet down. No such luck!

Frank's biggest problem is his temper. He can't ever seem to control his anger. When he gets mad, his younger brother and sister run for cover. In elementary school he frequently visited the principal's office. In high school he was disciplined twice for fighting. Now he has a job at a service station after school, and he's on probation for arguing with a customer.

Jody, David, and Frank have ADHD and they are having problems with social skills. They might benefit from social skills training. Social skills training involves educating people about social skills and teaching them to use learned skills in their social interactions. Through social skills training, kids can learn to advocate for themselves in different situations, deal with authority figures appropriately, maintain control over their behavior, initiate and carry on conversations, and show empathy and compassion for others to make friends.

Social skills training may be particularly important for children and adolescents with disabilities such as ADHD. People with ADHD may have more trouble holding conversations because they may not be able to listen attentively to a speaker or they may interrupt others. They have difficulty waiting their turn in games or in organized activities which require giving others a chance at equal participation. They may not be able to control their temper when they feel they have been wronged, causing them to lash out inappropriately. Social skills training can help them recognize when their behavior is inappropriate. The first step in teaching social skills is to do a social skills assessment.

Assessing a Student's Social Skills

The Tough Kid Social Skills Book by Susan M. Sheridan is an excellent resource for materials to help teachers assess students' social skills. Dr. Sheridan discusses three steps in the assessment process.

Step 1—Do a General Screening to Identify Students with Social Problems

The objective of this step is to identify students who teachers and peers recognize as having social problems.

Teacher nomination forms can be completed by teachers to identify students who: have few friends, frequently fight or argue with classmates, blame others for problems, do not show ability to solve problems cooperatively, fail to exhibit self-control, or are not well liked.

Sociograms can be completed by classmates. Similar to teacher nominations, sociograms are easy to administer. Each child in a classroom is asked to nominate three peers with whom they like to play or work and three peers with whom they would not like to play or work. Below are directions to make a sociogram of the students in a class.

1. Ask students to list the names of three classmates with whom they like to play.
2. Ask students to list the names of three classmates with whom they do *not* like to play.
3. Ask students to list the names of three classmates whom they would like to invite to a party or activity.
4. Ask students to list the names of three classmates whom they would like to *not* invite to a party or activity.

Count the number of times each student was listed in each of the activity categories. Based on the students' responses to the sociogram you could classify students in your class as either popular, rejected, neglected, or controversial.

Step 2—Use Rating Scales to Collect More In-Depth Information About a Student's Social Skills

There are several rating scales published to evaluate social skills. Rating scales are helpful because they can pinpoint a students' social skills strengths and weaknesses. Some examples of rating scales or books which contain such scales are:

- *Walker-McConnell Scale of Social Competence* (Elementary and Adolescent Versions) by Hill Walker and Scott R. McConnell
- *Social Skills Rating Scale (SSRS)* by Frank Gresham and Stephen Elliott
- *Skillstreaming in Early Childhood*, S*killstreaming the Elementary School Child*, and S*killstreaming the Adolescent* by Arnold P. Goldstein and Ellen McGinnis contain social skills inventories.
- *The Tough Kid Book* by Susan Sherian contains social skills inventories.

The Skills Survey (Sheridan, 1995) is an abbreviated rating scale for teachers. This brief scale can be used to identify social skills that could be targeted for training in a social skills training group. The items in the scale are rated from1 to 4 (never a problem to almost always a problem). Sample items are listed below:

- Noticing and Talking About Feelings   1 2 3 4
- Starting a Conversation   1 2 3 4
- Joining In   1 2 3 4
- Playing Cooperatively   1 2 3 4
- Keeping a Conversation Going   1 2 3 4
- Solving Problems   1 2 3 4
- Solving Arguments   1 2 3 4
- Dealing with Teasing   1 2 3 4
- Dealing with Being Left Out   1 2 3 4
- Using Self-Control   1 2 3 4
- Accepting "No"   1 2 3 4

Self-ratings by students can provide useful information about how students perceive their own social skills. However, many students with social difficulties attribute social problems to others and often deny or minimize social problems in themselves. Therefore, self-rating scales should be interpreted cautiously.

The *Skillstreaming* programs (Goldstein and McGinnis, 1997) have student manuals for elementary-age and adolescent students which contain very helpful self-rating scales. Below are examples of questions students are asked:

- Do I listen to someone who is talking to me?
- Do I start conversations with other people?
- Do I talk with other people about things that interest both of us?
- Do I introduce myself to new people?
- Do I ask for help when I am having difficulty?
- Do I help others who might need or want help?
- Do I pay full attention to whatever I am working on?
- Do I handle complaints made against me in a fair way?
- Do I deal positively with being left out of some activity?
- Do I stay in control when someone teases me?
- Do I control my temper when I feel upset?

Step 3—Interviewing Others and Observing Students

This step in the assessment process is the most costly and time consuming to do, but it often provides the most useful information about a child's social functioning. There are two procedures used in direct assessment: social skills interviews and direct observations of the student in the classroom, playground, cafeteria, and hallways at school.

Social skills interviews are conducted with parents, teachers, students, and peers. Parents may be asked about the specific concerns they have about their child's social skills, which concerns trouble them the most, what types of situations trigger problem behavior, etc. Students may be asked about the types of problems they have with peers, whether they are happy with their friendships, what areas they would like to improve, etc.

Through direct observation of the student in school, we can objectively measure the frequency with which students exhibit certain behavior. Direct observation of the student gives us first-hand data that cannot be collected through teacher nominations, sociograms, rating scales, or interviews. Some useful direct observation instruments are:

- *ADHD School Observation Code* by Kenneth Gadow, Joyce Sprafkin, and Edith Nolan (1996).
- *Social Skills Direct Observation Form* by Susan Sheridan (in *The Tough Kid Social Skills Book*, 1995).

When doing direct observation the observer watches the student and counts the number of times the student displays behavior described on the observation system. Observations are typically made during 15 second intervals and then recorded on a data sheet. For example when using the *Social Skills Direct Observation Form* the following social skills are rated:

Positive Social Behaviors
- Social Entry—student initiates social interaction
- Playing Cooperatively—student appropriately keeps an interaction going
- Solving Problems—student tries to manage conflict in an appropriate manner

Negative Social Behaviors
- Verbal Aggression—student makes threatening, negative remark or gesture
- Physical Aggression—student displays an overt, physical behavior that can inflict physical harm or damage
- Social Noncompliance—student displays behavior indicating defiance or intention of breaking a rule
- Isolated—student does not participate with others

Training Social Skills

For many years social skills were not taught in school in a systematic way. Teaching social skills was regarded as the parents' job rather than the teachers'. However, with the increase in child and adolescent aggression and violent behavior in our nation's schools and communities, programs were developed for educators to work with youth to improve self-control, social behavior, and build character. Youth now can receive group training to help them learn social skills. There are a number of social skills training programs commercially available.

Dr. Hill Walker and his colleagues developed a social skills program called *ACCESS* or the *Adolescent Curriculum for Communication and Effective Social Skills*. It was designed to teach 31 social skills in three areas: relating to peers, relating to adults, and relating to yourself. Specific skills across these areas include listening, greeting, offering assistance, getting an adult's attention, disagreeing with adults, following classroom rules, taking pride in your appearance, being organized, and using self-control.

One of the pioneers in the area of social skills training is Dr. Arnold P. Goldstein, who developed the *Prepare Curriculum* to teach children how to act and react in different social situations. With Ellen McGinnis, he developed the *Skillstreaming* program for early childhood, elementary, and adolescent age groups. *Skillstreaming the Adolescent* identifies 50 social skills within six different groups.

Social Skills in the *Skillstreaming the Adolescent* Program

Group 1: Beginning Social Skills
1. Listening
2. Starting a conversation
3. Having a conversation
4. Asking a question
5. Saying thank you
6. Introducing yourself
7. Introducing other people
8. Giving a compliment

Group II: Advanced Social Skills
9. Asking for help
10. Joining in
11. Giving instructions
12. Following instructions
13. Apologizing
14. Convincing others

Group III: Skills for Dealing with Feelings
15. Knowing your feelings
16. Expressing your feelings
17. Understanding feelings of others
18. Dealing with someone else's anger
19. Expressing affection
20. Dealing with fear
21. Rewarding yourself
22. Asking permission
23. Sharing something
24. Helping others
25. Negotiating

26. Using self-control
27. Standing up for your rights
28. Responding to teasing
29. Avoiding trouble with others
30. Keeping out of fights
31. Making a complaint
32 Answering a complaint
33. Being a good sport

Group V: Skills for Dealing with Stress
34. Dealing with embarrassment
35. Dealing with being left out
36. Standing up for a friend
37. Responding to persuasion
38. Responding to failure
39. Dealing with conflicting messages
40. Dealing with an accusation
41. Getting ready for a difficult conversation
42. Dealing with group pressure

Group VI: Planning Skills
43. Deciding on something to do
44. Deciding what caused a problem
45. Setting a goal
46. Deciding on your abilities
47. Gathering information
48. Prioritizing problems
49. Making a decision
50. Concentrating on a task

The core training procedures involved in the *Skillstreaming* program are modeling, role-playing, performance feedback, and generalization training. Trainers lead individuals in the group through nine steps to learn a skill, practice using it, and receive feedback from group members during role-play exercises.

A program called *Job-related Social Skills (JRSS)* covers a number of skills: prioritizing job responsibilities, understanding directions, giving instructions, asking questions, asking permission, asking for help, accepting help, offering help, requesting information, taking messages, engaging in a conversation, giving compliments, convincing others, apologizing, accepting criticism, and responding to complaints. Skills are taught using direct instruction, rehearsal, modeling, and role playing.

Dr. Berthold Berg has developed a series of games and workbooks that are designed to train social skills in older children and adolescents. His programs can be used with the guidance of a health care professional, educator, or parent. Dr. Berg identifies specific social skills and provides an inventory to assess the individual's current use of these skills in social interactions.

These are introduced to the child or adolescent in a game-like format and reinforced with a workbook the student can write in to strengthen skill knowledge. Through playing the game and completing the exercises in the workbook, children learn to identify the things they say to themselves during social interactions. They identify what Berg refers to as "negative self-talk," which he believes mediates behavior and causes us to act in negative ways to others or to ourselves. The games and exercises encourage children to replace negative self-talk with "positive self-talk," which is more constructive and likely to lead to self-confidence, better self-control, and positive interactions with others. His games and workbooks also focus on teaching children to say things to themselves that make them feel competent, expect success in what they try to do, not worry, accept making mistakes, give themselves credit, and compliment themselves.

In the *Social Skills Game* and the *Social Skills Workbook*, Berg lists four categories of skills containing specific behaviors under each:

Making friends	Responding positively to peers
Asking a question	Accepting a compliment
Giving a compliment	Helping peers in trouble
Introducing yourself	Offering help
Listening	Showing concern for peer
Starting a conversation	Standing up for peers

Cooperating with peers	Communicating needs
Following rules	Asking for help
Joining in	Asking to borrow another's property
Sharing	Expressing negative feelings
Suggesting an activity	Expressing positive feelings
Taking turns	Getting attention appropriately

Generalization of Skill Training to the Real World

Teaching children and adolescents social skills is not difficult. Getting them to apply what they have learned and to use these skills in the real world is another matter. The results have been disappointing.

To be socially competent, a person must be able to determine when a social skill would be appropriate to use in a given social situation *and* must be motivated to use it. Social skill problems can be the result of an acquisition deficit or a performance deficit. An acquisition deficit is a problem which is the result of a person not knowing what to do within a social situation. A performance deficit is a problem which is the result of a person not doing what he knows.

After receiving social skills training, a child may know what skill to use and how to use it within a given social situation, but may fail to use the skill correctly, if at all. If they have ADHD, they may not be able to regulate their behavior sufficiently to use the social skill—even if they know what it is.

For example, a child with ADHD may know the appropriate negotiation skill to use to ask his parent for permission to stay out past his curfew. He may not, however, be capable of controlling his frustration if his parent doesn't grant permission. At the slightest sign of a negative response, the ADHD adolescent's emotions may erupt into an aggressive attack. The parent may respond aggressively, and the conversation erupts into an argument. Instead of giving permission to stay out later, the parent may punish the teen by grounding him that night.

Many social skills training programs contains strategies designed to increase the likelihood that a trainee will use the social skill in daily life. In the *Skillstreaming* program, Arnold Goldstein

109

and Ellen McGinnis provide training to parents as well as the kids. Parent training groups meet separately from the kid's group. Parents are instructed to use the trained social skill in the presence of their son or daughter. They strengthen the skill for their child by modeling. Parents are also trained to give praise when they observe a social skill being used properly.

How Parents Can Promote Positive Social Skills

- Serve as good role models and behave in socially appropriate ways. Children and adolescents learn what they live. Parents who model appropriate social behavior are more likely to promote appropriate social behavior in their children. This is particularly true when a specific social skill is targeted for learning. Make an effort to model use of the social skill as much as possible.

- Recognize when the child is using a social skill well and provide positive reinforcement to the child. This will strengthen the use of the social skill in the future.

- Calmly and constructively point out inappropriate social behavior and suggest a more appropriate replacement behavior. It is important to couch reminders in a positive, non-condescending way.

- Encourage the child to use problem-solving strategies. Through use of the problem-solving strategies children could learn to successfully resolve potential conflicts with peers in an appropriate manner.

How Teachers Can Promote Positive Social Skills

- Students with ADHD often are not aware of how their behavior affects others. Some will talk incessantly about a favorite topic, not realizing others are no longer interested. Some will overreact to situations and become oblivious to how foolish they appear to others. Teachers may be able to strengthen prosocial behavior by pointing out examples of positive interaction and praising.

• Monitor social interactions to gain clearer sense of student's behavior with others.

• Set up social behavior goals with student and implement a social skills program.

• Prompt appropriate social behavior either verbally or with a private signal.

• Encourage student to observe a classmate who exhibits appropriate social skills.

• Avoid placing student in competitive activities where there is a greater likelihood of stress leading to negative social behavior.

• Encourage cooperative learning tasks.

• Provide small group social skills training in-class or through related services using a systematic program.

• Praise student to increase esteem to others.

• Assign special responsibilities to student in presence of peers to elevate status in class.

• Pair students instead of letting students choose.

• Encourage participation in after school "clubs" and activities.

111

Helping Students Develop Empathy, Self-control, and Cooperativeness

Empathy toward others, self-control, and cooperativeness are core social skills. Many ingredients that go into forming good friendships involve the ability of a person to show empathy and self-control and to display a cooperative attitude towards others. Below is a questionnaire that will help students identify their strengths or weaknesses in these areas (Davis, et al. 1996):

Read each of the statements below and rate whether the statement describes you:

Yes	No	Empathy
___	___	1. I show sympathy for others.
___	___	2. I am considerate of others' feelings.
___	___	3. I am a good listener.
___	___	4. I go out of my way to show a helpful attitude to others.

		Self-control
___	___	5. I show self-control in difficult situations.
___	___	6. I can accept constructive criticism from others.
___	___	7. I stay calm when things don't go my way.
___	___	8. It takes a lot for me to get angry.

		Cooperativeness
___	___	9. I make friends easily.
___	___	10. I can keep a conversation going.
___	___	11. I invite others to participate in activities.
___	___	12. I compliment others on their work, appearance, etc.

If the student had three or more "Yes" answers in each category he or she probably communicates well with other students. If the student had less than three "Yes" answers in any of the categories, improvement in that area is needed. We have included exercises on the following pages to help students.

Exercise—Increasing Empathy Toward Others

Empathy is the act of showing consideration, sympathy, and sensitivity to the needs of others. Empathy towards someone else can be shown by our words, facial expressions, body language, and our behavior towards others. When we show empathy towards others, we are saying to someone else, "I understand what you're going through and I care about you." We usually show empathy towards others to provide support when someone is going through a difficult time. Needless to say, showing consideration to others and being sensitive to their feelings help build strong relationships.

Directions: Follow these steps to improve your ability to show empathy to others:

1. Figure out how the person is feeling, i.e., sad, angy, nervous, worried, etc. Watch the other person when they are describing their situation. Notice facial expressions, tone of voice, and body movements. They all give you clues about how this person is feeling.
2. Listen carefully to what the person is saying. Try to follow the content of what they are saying.
3. Decide on ways to show that you understand what the person is feeling such as through a gentle touch or a concerned look or gesture.
4. Review the examples below of statements and actions which do or do not show empathy.

Examples of statements which show empathy:
- "You seem upset."
- "I understand how you feel."
- "I can imagine how that must be for you."
- "It sounds like you're going through a rough time."
- "I see what you're saying."
- "I understand."
- "I know what you mean."

Actions which do not show empathy:
- offering unsolicited advice
- showing disapproval or disrespect
- responding in a judgmental way
- being long-winded
- taking sides
- changing the topic

- looking away while the person is talking
- showing disinterest in the other person
- "If you think you've had it rough, listen to me. My story is worse."

<u>Role Play and Discussion</u>
- A good way to practice showing empathy is to role play a conversation. Two or more students can play different parts and be involved in the role playing while other students try to identify statements or behaviors which show empathy.
- Example: A student was counting on getting a job in the mall this summer. His application was turned down and he's worried he won't be able to find another job.
- Discussing real-life situations when showing empathy helps form and strengthen a relationship

Exercise—Increasing Self-Control

Self-control is the ability to control one's behavior and emotions under stressful conditions. Self-control is shown by calmness in our voice and behavior as we react in an even-tempered way without emotional extremes of anger, sadness, or frustration.

<u>Directions: Follow these steps when faced with a stressful situation.</u>
1. Give yourself time to "cool off" before reacting.
2. Keep your thoughts and your body calm.
3. Think about your choices and make logical decisions.

Common statements people say to themselves to keep in control:
- I can work this out.
- I can handle this situation.
- Relax and think this through.
- Stay calm. Breathe easily. Just continue to relax.
- I'm not going to let this thing get the best of me.
- I can stay in control.
- Getting upset won't help anything.
- Don't worry. Things will work out for the best.
- There is no point in getting mad.

- A good way to practice self-control is through role playing and modeling behavior. Two or more students can

114

act out a stressful situation demonstrating different methods of showing self-control. Other students can identify other methods of self-control that can be used.

- Discuss examples of real-life situations when self-control could have made for a better outcome in a situation.

Exercise—Increasing Cooperativeness

Cooperativeness is the act of showing cooperation to get along with others. Cooperativeness is shown by being helpful, waiting one's turn, sharing, trusting others, listening to others, and following instructions. When we show cooperativeness we are working or playing alongside others in a helpful, positive way.

Directions: Follow these steps to show cooperativeness:
1. Determine if the other person may need and want help before offering help. Use verbal, facial, and behavioral cues to judge whether someone needs help (person asks for help, looks puzzled, looks as if he is struggling).
2. When playing a game or sport, show respect for the other person. Follow the rules of the game or sport. Determine who starts and wait for your turn. Congratulate the other person if he won or tell the other person he did well, even if he lost.
3. When working on a project with others, show respect for them. Determine each person's part in the project and make certain to do your share as best you can. Offer help to others, wait your turn when speaking, and be considerate of others' feelings when making comments.

Summary

Many children with ADHD would benefit from learning and using appropriate social skills. Social behavior is often inappropriate in those with ADHD. Hyperactive-impulsive people tend to interrupt others, shift topics in conversations, intrude into other's "space," and have difficulty controlling behavior and emotions. Other people notice this behavior within a short time of meeting someone with ADHD and quickly form a negative impression. People with ADHD—inattentive type, tend to be more quiet and passive. They would benefit from learning and using social skills that would enable them to communicate more assertively.

There are a number of social skills training programs available. These programs are usually run in small social skills groups and are offered in schools or in counseling settings. Parents can reinforce the use of social skills by appropriately modeling skills to their child and by praising positive behavior.

Chapter 9

Strategies to Help Students
Who Have Problems with Homework

Why is Homework Important?

Homework has probably been around for as long as schools have been in existence. The purpose of homework is to reinforce and further the education of students.

It is common for students to have difficulties with homework. As many as one-fourth of students in general education and more than half of students in special education have trouble with homework. About half of all high school students complete less than 80 percent of their homework. Boredom is usually the number one reason children cite for not doing their homework.

Homework is often a source of significant stress for students, parents, and teachers alike. Students complain that their homework is often boring, difficult, and takes too long to complete. They would rather be socializing or watching television. Parents complain that they do not always understand the purpose of their child's homework and are confused about how much they should be involved in working with their child on homework. Teachers are frustrated when students don't complete homework or when they show a lack of interest in doing homework. They also spend a lot of valuable time checking and correcting homework. Time which some feel could be better spent on instruction.

Despite the problems with homework, teachers and parents realize the importance that homework plays in education. In their book, *Seven Steps to Homework Success,* Sydney Zentall and Sam Goldstein point out several constructive purposes for homework.

1. Through practice and participation in learning tasks, homework will improve a student's achievement in

117

general academic areas such as reading, writing, spelling, and mathematics, and in knowledge areas such as history and science.

2. A student's sense of responsibility can be strengthened through the homework process. The student must bring assignments home, organize work materials, complete assignments in a certain time, and return assignments to school to receive a grade. Organizational skills, planning, and time management are learned through this process.

3. Homework can strengthen a parent's relationship with their child if things go smoothly. Through the homework process parents have an opportunity to support their child's efforts, work together on meaningful projects, and establish a positive parent-child alliance.

4. For teachers, homework is a cost-effective way to deliver instruction.

5. Homework provides a method by which teachers can show parents what their child is learning in school.

- Homework helps learning and its importance increases as children move into middle school and high school.

- For elementary-aged students, homework should foster positive attitudes toward school and provide a link between home experiences and school learning.

- Students in elementary school need high levels of feedback and/or supervision with homework so they can practice their assignments correctly. Students in higher grades will benefit from homework even if less supervision and

118

less frequent feedback from teachers or parents is provided.

- Students who devote time to homework are probably on
a path to improved achievement. The table below indi-
cates a guideline as to the amount of time students in
grades 1-12 should spend on homework (Zentall &
Goldstein, 1999).

Time Spent on Homework		
Grade	# Assignments	Time Required
1 to 3	1-3 per week	15 minutes
4 to 6	2-4 per week	15-45 minutes
7 to 9	3-5 sets per week	45-75 minutes per set
10 to 12	4-5 sets per week	75-150 minutes per set

- Homework should not be given as a punishment. Make
sure homework that is assigned is relevant to the learning needs of the student.

- The most frequently assigned types of homework are:
unfinished classwork (51%); practice (22%); enrichment
or make-up work (9%); and preparation for upcoming
classwork (6%) or for a test (4%) (Zentall & Goldstein,
1999).

- The focus today is on student discovery and understanding through experiences. Therefore, teachers may be
more creative in their homework assignments than in the
past in an effort to help the student develop critical thinking skills and come up with their own ideas in problem-
solving.

Teachers, complete the checklist below to assess whether you follow the following positive teacher homework practices suggested by Drs. Zentall and Goldstein.

Checklist of Positive Teacher Homework Practices

Yes	No	Do you make sure students have assignment books, homework planners, or homework buddies?
Yes	No	Do you make daily assignments at the beginning of the class rather than at the end?
Yes	No	Do you make sure your students understand the directions they are given about homework by asking them to repeat them or by checking what is written in assignment books?
Yes	No	Do you present instructions visually (overheads, on the board) as well as orally?
Yes	No	Do you help students who have trouble organizing their materials at the end of the period or end of the day?
Yes	No	Do you help students who have trouble attending by reducing the amount of homework assigned?
Yes	No	Do you try to make homework interesting to students?
Yes	No	Do you talk about the purpose of an assignment?
Yes	No	Do you avoid giving homework that requires self-teaching or new learning?
Yes	No	Do you allow students to practice some homework problems in class to make sure they understand how to do an assignment before taking it home?
Yes	No	Do you allow students with handwriting difficulties to use computers or tape recorders to reduce writing and copying?
Yes	No	Do you provide rewards for students who complete homework?
Yes	No	Do you have students turn in a written excuse for missed assignments?

- At the beginning of the school year explain your homework policy to students and to parents in a letter to be brought home.

- Do not introduce *new* material as homework. Homework should be independent practice of a skill covered in class, a review of material already presented, or an enrichment activity to build on skills already covered.

- Write homework assignments in addition to giving them orally.

- Inform parents immediately if a student is having chronic homework problems.

- Instruct parents on the following general strategies they can use at home to help their child build positive homework habits.
  - ✓ set a time each day for homework to be done
  - ✓ set a place in which the child is to do homework
  - ✓ make certain the child has materials to complete homework (i.e., pens, pencils, paper, books, etc.)
  - ✓ be available to answer questions and provide guidance and support, but do not offer too much help
  - ✓ review homework to make certain your child has completed (or at least attempted to complete) everything assigned, but do not check for accuracy in detail
  - ✓ for younger children, check that they bring homework to school the next day.

- Take other teacher's assignments into account when assigning homework yourself.

- Make certain the instructions you provide to students about homework are clear. The additional time it will take you to carefully review what you expect may save students from an entire night of confusion.

- Before the end of the class period, or at the end of the day, review the homework assignments once again. Remind students what books and materials they will need at home to complete assignments.

121

- Check homework at the start of class on the day it is due. Students become frustrated if teachers don't check homework that they spent time doing.

- Keep track of grades—give immediate feedback about test scores.

- Encourage student to put completed work in specific folder.

- Have student check school work that is due the evening before.

- Use a homework lottery to motivate students to do homework. All students who successfully complete homework for the day put their names on a small card that is dropped in a jar. On Friday, a drawing is held, selecting one or more winners. Winners could receive prizes or privileges. One such prize may be a "no homework pass" which the student redeem at any time to be excused from one night's homework.

- Teacher should call parent if three assignments are missing.

Suggestions for Common Homework Problems

1. When a student regularly fails to complete homework assignments.
    a. Talk to the student about why homework was not completed.
    b. Provide assistance to the student if needed in the form of peer tutoring, aids, checking more frequently, etc.
    c. Give fewer assignments or cut the assignment length.
    d. Make adaptations in assignments (alternative formats).

e. Require parent signatures on homework assignments.

f. Send notes home.

g. Be flexible on late work turned in and give partial credit.

h. Have the student maintain list of other students' phone numbers to get work.

i. Provide long-term outline of assignments and due dates.

j. Mail home assignments for next several weeks or use e-mail or Internet web site.

k. Give parents access to teacher's school phone number and free period.

l. Prepare a written contract with student to complete work.

m. Evaluate effectiveness of medication with student's doctor.

2. When a student rushes through homework and makes errors.

a. Instruct parents to review their child's homework assignments each night and check for accuracy and completeness.

b. In class, individually review with the child how you expect the homework assignment to be done. Go over directions and have the child highlight key words.

c. Instruct parents to withhold privileges (television, play, phone, etc.) until a certain amount of homework is completed and checked for accuracy.

d. If handwriting is a problem for the child, seek alternatives to lengthy writing assignments.

3. When a student avoids homework because of a lack of confidence.

a. Individually review the assignment with the student in class to make sure the child understands it. Have the student do one or two examples with you to make certain the child is not confused.

  b. Shorten the assignment so the student does not feel overwhelmed.

  c. Instruct the parents to be supportive and complimentary to the child when an effort is made to do homework.

4.   When a student takes too long to complete homework.

  a. If the child has trouble staying on task long enough to complete homework the parent should try giving breaks.

  b. Set up short-term goals for homework completion. For example, have the child estimate how much time it will take to do each part of his/her homework. Then encourage the child to stick to the time schedule set up and offer breaks when appropriate. Reward the child for satisfactorily sticking to their schedule.

  c. While the child is doing homework, focus your attention on the positive aspects of the child's behavior. Notice when your child is on-task and praise appropriately. Avoid nagging your child to "get to work" when he is off task.

  d. Withhold preferred activities (e.g., television time, socializing, use of phone) until homework goals are accomplished.

5.   When a student has difficulty with long-term projects:

  a. Break projects into smaller parts and prepare a time line for each part.

  b. Work with parents at home to organize when work segments are to be completed.

  c. Use a "month-at-a-glance" calendar to track long-term assignments.

Effective Home-School Communication Practices

- Establish effective communication with parents about their child's homework practices. As indicated earlier, homework provides a picture to the parent of what their child is learning in school. However, communication through homework alone is not sufficient for students who are struggling in school. Active and frequent parent-teacher communication is a very effective strategy to help stuggling students, especially if homework is an issue.

- One of the most frequent methods parents and teachers use to communicate is home-notes. Daily notes have been shown to yield very positive benefits to students with improvements in work completed, behavior, and academic performance. Home-notes can vary in detail, but the important thing is that both parents and teachers be consistent in reading and writing each other's thoughts and suggestions to help the student.

Sample Home-Note

Name:_____   Date:_____

Behavior	Effort	Progress	
__Positive	__ Good	__Satisfactory	
__Satisfactory	__Satisfactory	__Unsatisfactory	
__Occasionally poor	__Minimal	__Improving	
__Frequently poor	__Declining	__Declining	

Homework	Test Scores	Work	Social
__Completed well	__Good	__Exceptional	__Positive
__Adequate	__Average	__Adequate	__Fair
__Unprepared	__Poor	__Poor	__Very Poor

Teacher's Comments and Signature

Parent's Comments and Signature

125

- Encourage parents to employ the following homework guidelines:

  a. Set up a homework schedule that lets the child know when homework is to be started. Some children cannot decide when to sit down and do homework on their own. They need their parent to make that decision for them. During homework time there should be no phone calls taken, no television, and no interruptions.

  b. Parents should not sit near their child during homework time. Sitting nearby merely increases the likelihood that the child will become dependent on the parent for help with homework. When this happens a child will become unable to do homework unless the parent is nearby. When the parent moves away, the work tends to stop. Advise parents not to get in the habit of sitting near their child who is doing homework.

  c. When checking homework, advise parents to give praise for correct problems first then encourage the child to look over incorrect ones and see if the child can come up with a "different answer."

  d. Some children will linger over their homework for many hours without making progress. When this occurs, parents should not let homework drag on all night. Stop after a reasonable time and offer to write a note to the teacher explaining the problem.

  e. When the child is not sure of how to solve a group of problems, have the child do a few and then check those completed for accuracy. In this way the child gets immediate feedback about the correctness of his work.

  f. Parents should be advised not to finish their child's homework assignments. Some parents will do the entire assignment for their child. While the parent may be well-intentioned, doing this can be very destructive. It can foster feelings of inadequacy in the child and makes the child dependent on the parent.

Summary

Many students have problems with understanding and completing homework. Students with ADHD often spend hours doing assignments which should only take minutes to complete. Problems with attention span (especially if they are not taking medication after school) is one of the main reasons students with ADHD have so many homework problems. In addition, they may have trouble writing down and organizing assignments and they may forget or lose material necessary to bring home to complete homework.

Teachers should follow appropriate practices in assigning homework to students. For students with ADHD or other problems specific accommodations can be made to help the students organize, plan, and execute homework. Teachers should also advise parents on positive homework practices they can follow at home to enable the student to work independently on homework.

Chapter 10
A Quick Reference Guide
to Medications for ADHD

Medicine has been used to treat ADHD for more than five decades. The research on medical treatments for ADHD is abundant and it clearly shows the efficacy of stimulant medications to treat symptoms of this disorder. The benefits have carefully been measured against the risks. The conclusion is that many children (70-90 percent) diagnosed with ADHD will be helped by medication. In some cases, medication will be the most effective treatment they will receive.

The most comprehensive study to date (the MTA study) investigated the effect of different treatments given to 579 children ages 7 to 9.9 years who were diagnosed with ADHD, combined type. Children were divided into four treatment groups. One group was assigned to a *medication-only* treatment wherein they received carefully adjusted stimulant medication which was monitored every month by their doctor with the help of parents and teachers who rated the child's behavior and attention. A second group of children and their parents received a very comprehensive *psychosocial treatment program* to improve behavior, attention, social skills, and academic performance. Parents in this group attended thirty-five sessions of parent training to learn about ADHD and to acquire skills to manage child behavior. Children in this group were followed in school by a paraprofessional, received daily report cards to evaluate school behavior, and attended an intensive summer training program designed to teach social skills and self-control. A third group of children received a *combination* of carefully controlled medication and the comprehensive psychosocial treatments described above. A fourth group, the *community control group*, was sent back into the community and instructed to get treatment for their child.

The results of this study are still being evaluated. However, after fourteen months of treatment it was clear that the combination group that received both medication and psychosocial treatments improved the most in terms of core symptoms of ADHD (attention, hyperactivity, and impulsivity) as well as in overall performance. The group that did second best was the one that received medication only. Medication seemed to have the strongest impact on the core symptoms of ADHD. Children who received psychosocial treatments alone did less well. Those who did the poorest were the children who were sent into the community to receive treatment.

The MTA study was the largest study ever done of ADHD treatments and has led experts to draw many conclusions about treatment. Below are three main points often cited.

1. Medication plus behavioral treatments work best for children with ADHD. Children with ADHD should receive multi-modal therapy.

2. Medication alone can be quite effective in reducing core symptoms of ADHD—inattention, impulsivity, and hyperactivity.

3. Medication was most effective when it was carefully adjusted to the needs of the child. Most children in the medication groups were monitored more frequently and treated with medication more vigorously than those in the community treatment group as they received higher daily doses generally given three times per day.

- Physicians need the cooperation of parents and school personnel to ensure that the medication is needed, that main effects and side effects are monitored, and that it is available and is taken by the student as prescribed.

- Parents and school personnel should be responsible for giving medication to the student. Some youngsters will forget to take scheduled doses of medication, others may be resistant to taking medication either because they don't like the way it tastes, they have trouble swallowing a pill, or they don't like the way they feel when the medication is working.

• Teachers should be discreet when reminding a student to take medication in school. Taking medication is the student's private business, and it should not be made public! Long acting medications which are now available may greatly reduce the need for in-school dosing.

• Medication should never be given without an established system to monitor its effectiveness. The doctor prescribing the medication should obtain information from parents and teachers. Typically, teachers are the best source of information about medication effects on the student with ADHD. Teachers may report information about the student's reactions to medication informally to the physician or they may complete similar forms as the parents for more systematic data collection. Use of behavior rating scales such as the *Conners Teacher Rating Scale-Revised* (Conners, 1997) or similar scales can be extremely helpful in determining changes in behavior.

The ADHD Monitoring System developed by Dr. David Rabiner is a convenient program that parents can use to carefully monitor how their child is doing at school. By using this program, parents will be able to carefully track their child's progress in school and will be alerted as to when any adjustments or modifications to their child's treatment need to be discussed with their physician.

Parents and the child should report information about medication reactions to the physician. This will give the physician an idea of how well the medication is working and if there are any adverse side effects.

• If a child has been taking medication for ADHD for awhile, it is a good idea to have a no-medication trial in which behavior off medication could be observed by parents and teachers.

Stimulants

There have been more than 150 controlled studies on the use of stimulant medications to treat ADHD. Some of the most frequently used stimulants are Adderall, Ritalin, Focalin, Metadate, Methylin, and Dexedrine. Concerta, Adderall XR, Metadate CD, Focalin LA, and Focalin XR release methylphenidate (or amphetamine salts in the case of Adderall XR) over an eight to twelve hour period. They use special delivery systems which regulate the release of active medication to last longer than standard short-term preparations. In April 2006, the Food and Drug Administration approved Daytrana, the first transdermal (skin) patch, for treating ADHD in children six to 12 years of age. Daytrana is a once daily treatment containing methylphenidate,

Stimulants are the first-line medications used for ADHD. Their effectiveness (at least for the short-term) in treating ADHD has been demonstrated in more than 50 years of clinical use in a large number of patients and in hundreds of studies. Stimulants are the first choice of many clinicians treating ADHD because they work quickly (usually within 30 to 60 minutes), most side effects are mild and reversible, dosing can be modified for optimum results, the effects can be seen within hours, and abuse of stimulants is uncommon.

- Stimulants increase brain activity or arousal. This enables the brain to do a better job of inhibiting behavior and attending to tasks. The stimulants do this by improving the way certain neurotransmitter chemicals work. When stimulants act on the brain to cause the release of dopamine (and/or to inhibit the reuptake of dopamine in the synapse) for example, the brain is better able to inhibit behavior and maintain attention.

- In addition to improving hyperactivity, impulsivity, and inattention, stimulants can positively affect academic performance, eye-hand coordination, and social behavior. Teachers often report improvements in the work habits of hyperactive students on stimulant medication. They get their work done quicker, more accurately, and neater

132

than before. They also see a change in social behavior with less interruptions in class and better cooperation with peers and teachers. For some children, stimulant medication reduces aggressive behavior and defiance.

• To follow is a list of documented effects of stimulant medicines on children with ADHD.
  ✓ reduced activity level to normal
  ✓ decreased excessive talking and disruption in classroom
  ✓ improved handwriting and neatness of written work
  ✓ improved fine motor control
  ✓ improved attention to tasks
  ✓ reduced distractibility
  ✓ improved short-term memory
  ✓ decreased impulsivity
  ✓ increased academic productivity (i.e., work produced)
  ✓ increased accuracy of academic work
  ✓ reduced off-task behavior in classroom
  ✓ decreased anger, better self-control
  ✓ improved participation in organized sports (i.e., baseball)
  ✓ reduced bossy behavior with peers
  ✓ reduced verbal and physical aggression with peers
  ✓ improved peer social status
  ✓ reduced non-compliant, defiant, and oppositional behavior
  ✓ improved parent-child interactions
  ✓ improved teacher-student interactions

• The long-term effects of stimulants have not been carefully studied, but in the MTA study, the behavioral and cognitive effects of stimulants were monitored over a 24 month period—a relatively short term considering people with ADHD take stimulants for years. Nevertheless, findings from the MTA study showed significant

133

reduction in core symptoms of ADHD (inattention, hyperactivity, impulsivity) and associated problems of aggression and oppositional behavior as measured by teacher ratings and parent ratings.

- In the early 1980s only about 40 percent of ADHD children in elementary school on stimulants continued taking stimulants in secondary school. Ten years later, more than 90 percent of children with ADHD continued to be prescribed stimulants during adolescence. There have only been a handful of published studies investigating the effects of stimulant treatment in adolescents. Those that have been done lead us to expect that stimulant treatments work equally well for children and adolescents.

- There is no evidence that children build up a significant tolerance to stimulants even after taking them for years throughout childhood and adolescence. When children move from elementary school to middle school, their school functioning may worsen. Some practitioners assume the adolescents may have developed a tolerance to their medication or may need more medication due to increases in physical size and weight. The physician's response is to prescribe a larger dose or change the medication to find something more effective. It may be better to investigate how accommodations can be made to assist the child in school first before making a change in medication.

- It is generally safe to take most other medications while taking stimulants. However, parents should check with a physician to be certain.

- There is little evidence to support any widespread abuse of methylphenidate. There are no cases of methylphenidate abuse or dependence in the over 150 controlled studies of stimulants in children, adolescents, or adults with ADHD. Parents should not be overly concerned that the use of a stimulant medication such as Ritalin for treatment of ADHD would lead to dependence, addiction, or drug abuse. However, misuse/abuse of stimulants can and does occur and parents should be aware of this. There have been fairly frequent reports of elementary and secondary school children giving away or selling stimulants such as Ritalin, reports of diversion of Ritalin into the hands of family members and teachers, and attempts by people to secure Ritalin through unlawful prescriptions. Parents should maintain possession of any stimulant medication at home and carefully monitor the supply. The school should do so as well for medication dispensed during the school day. Hopefully, use of long-acting stimulants given once a day will reduce this problem.

- Common side effects of the stimulants are:
  - headaches
  - stomachaches
  - insomnia
  - irritability
  - appetite loss
  - weight loss

- About half of the children started on a stimulant will experience one or more of the common side effects noted above. Interestingly, this same percentage of ADHD children will complain about similar side effects when they take a placebo pill without any active medication. Stomachaches and headaches occur in about one third of children taking a stimulant. Decreased appetite occurs often and usually results in the child eating little for lunch due to the morning dose of medication. If a second or third dose is taken midday or later, this could affect appetite at dinner as well. For most children, however, their appetite returns after school, and they easily make up for the missed lunchtime meal. Parents should consult their doctor if appetite suppression is chronic and the weight loss is significant. Medication dose or timing may need to be modified, nutritional supplements can be added to the diet, or serving a hearty breakfast or late night snack may help.

• Some of the infrequent side effects that can be caused by stimulant use include rebound effects, difficulty falling asleep, irritable mood, and tics. These side effects have not been well researched in adolescents, but are well understood in children.

• *Rebound.* Some parents report that at the end of the school day, their child becomes more hyperactive, excitable, talkative, and irritable. This phenomena is referred to as "rebound," and it can affect many children with ADHD who take stimulant medication during the school day. When rebound occurs, it usually begins after the last dose of medication is wearing off. The doctor may recommend a smaller dose of medication be given or use of another medication to reduce the child's excitability. Rebound may be less common when using long-acting stimulants such as Concerta, Adderall XR, Focalin LA, or Metadate CD.

• *Difficulty falling asleep.* ADHD children taking stimulants who have trouble falling asleep may be experiencing a drug rebound, which makes it difficult for them to quiet down and become restful. In some cases the doctor may recommend reducing the midday dose of medication or may prescribe a small dose of stimulant medication before bedtime. Other medications such as Clonidine or Benadryl may be prescribed to help the child fall asleep.

• *Irritability.* Clinicians and researchers both have noted that stimulant usage in ADHD children may worsen the child's mood. The child may exhibit more frequent temper outbursts, may be more moody, and may become more easily frustrated than usual. Moodiness could lead to much more oppositional behavior at home, greater sibling conflict, and conflicts with peers. Stimulants can also produce dysphoria (sadness) in some children. If irritability or sadness becomes a concern, the doctor may first try lowering the dose of stimulant, switch to a different stimulant, or may try a different class of medication altogether such as an antidepressant medication to treat the ADHD and mood problems.

- *Tics and Tourette's syndrome.* Simple motor tics consist of small, abrupt muscle movements usually around the face and upper body. Common simple motor tics include eye blinking, neck jerking, shoulder shrugging, and facial grimacing. Common simple vocal tics include throat clearing, grunting, sniffing, and snorting. Stimulants should be used with caution in patients with motor or vocal tics or in patients with a family history of tics. A little more than half of the ADHD children who start treatment with a stimulant medication will develop a subtle, transient motor or vocal tic. The tic might begin immediately or months after the medication is started. It might disappear on its own while the child is taking stimulants or it might worsen. Many physicians prefer to discontinue or reduce the stimulant medication if tics appear.

A child who has either a motor or a vocal tic (but not both), which occurs many times a day, nearly every day, for a period of at least one year (without stopping for more than three months), may be diagnosed as having a chronic tic disorder. Tourette's syndrome is a chronic tic disorder characterized by <u>both</u> multiple motor tics and one or more vocal tics. These tics are more severe than the simple motor tics described above. They involve the head and, frequently, other parts of the body such as the torso, arms, and legs. Vocal tics may include the production of sounds like clucking, grunting, yelping, barking, snorting, and coughing. Coprolalia, the utterance of obscenities, is rare and occurs in about 10 percent of children with Tourette's. Stimulants should be used cautiously with children who have chronic tic disorder or Tourette's syndrome and ADHD.

* *Cardiovascular effects and seizure threshold.* There has been some speculation and concern that stimulant medications may produce adverse cardiovascular effects in children, particularly with long term use. While stimulants may cause some elevation of the heart rate in some children with ADHD, there is no evidence of any long term cardiovascular effects. Furthermore, there is no evidence that stimulants lower the seizure threshold putting the child at greater risk for having a seizure.

* Is Ritalin and other stimulants overprescribed in the U.S.? Are they being used as a "quick fix" by parents, doctors, and teachers? There has been a dramatic increase in the prescribing of many psychotropic medications to treat disorders in children, not only those suffering from ADHD. Research and clinical experience has shown that children with anxiety, depression, and other disorders can benefit from the same medicines that help adults with these conditions.

The best and most current study on the number of children in the U.S. who are being prescribed Ritalin has been done by Dr. Daniel Safer and his colleagues. Dr. Safer found that approximately 1.5 million children take medication to treat ADHD. This amounts to between 3 and 4 percent of the 40 million school-age children. This seems to be within the range expected since it is conservatively estimated that ADHD probably affects from 3-5 percent of children. To avoid inappropriate prescribing of medication, careful evaluations of children suspected of having ADHD should be done.

Non-Stimulants to Treat ADHD

There is no doubt that stimulants are safe and effective in the treatment of ADHD and that they are generally considered the first-line medication to use. However, not all children will show an adequate response to stimulants, some may develop adverse side effects, and others may benefit from a medication that has twenty-four hour effectiveness rather than the limited coverage that stimulants can provide. In addition, the fact that stimulants are controlled substances, worries some parents who would like an alternative medication.

Atomoxetine (Strattera) has been marketed for the past several years as an FDA approved treatment for ADHD in children and in adults. It is a selective norepinephrine reuptake inhibitor (SNRI) and as such it blocks the reuptake of norepinephrine in certain regions of the brain. It is administered in the morning (or at night if the child becomes too sedated) and the dose is based on body weight. The starting dose is 0.5 mg/kg and the target daily dose might be 1.2 mg/kg. Strattera comes in capsules of 10, 18, 25, 40, and 60 mg strengths. It could take four to six weeks (or more) to reach maximal effect, however, the effects last twenty-four hours a day. It is sometimes used in combination with stimulants. In children, the side effects most likely to be seen with Strattera include stomach aches, sedation, nausea and vomiting, loss of appetite and headaches.

Tricyclic Antidepressants

Tricyclic antidepressants (TCAs) are primarily used in children for ADHD and tic disorders. They are regarded as alternatives for children who have not succeeded with stimulants, for whom stimulants produced unacceptable side effects, or who suffer from other conditions (such as depression, anxiety, Tourette's syndrome, tics), or aggressive behavior and irritability along with ADHD. Imi-

139

pramine (Tofranil), desipramine (Norpramin), amytriptyline (Elavil), and nortriptyline (Pamelor or Vivactyl), doxepin, and clomipramine (Anafranil) are TCAs.

- TCAs have the advantage of longer duration of action (all day) as opposed to four to eight hours common to stimulants. This avoids the troublesome and even embarrassing midday stimulant dose taken at school.

- Unfortunately, TCAs may not be as effective as the stimulants in improving attention and concentration or reducing hyperactive-impulsive symptoms of ADHD.

- TCAs also can produce adverse side effects, the most common of which are drowsiness, dry mouth, constipation, and abdominal discomfort. More concern, however, has been expressed at possible adverse cardiac side effects, accidental overdose, and reduced effectiveness over time.

- Because of their short half-life, stimulants are washed out of the body, or at least substantially reduced, within several hours after the last dose was taken. TCAs, however, have a longer half-life and remain in the bloodstream for a greater period of time. Levels of drugs can build to a point where a toxic amount is present causing irritability, excitability, agitation, anger, aggression, confusion, forgetfulness, or more serious health risks. By drawing blood, levels of the TCA can be measured to determine whether these symptoms are a result of too much medication in the body or other factors related to the patient's illness.

Noradrenergic Agonists

Noradrenergic agonists such as clonidine (Catapres) and guanfacine (Tenex) have been found to be useful in the treatment of ADHD children, especially those who are extremely hyperactive, excitable, impulsive, and defiant. They have less effectiveness in improving attention. They are often the drug of choice in treating children with tics or children who did not respond to stimulants. Clonidine is also prescribed to help children who have difficulty falling asleep. It can be a great benefit to children with sleep onset difficulties whether the cause is ADHD overarousal, stimulant medication rebound, or unwillingness to fall asleep.

- Clonidine comes in a tablet form or in a skin patch. The skin patch may be useful to improve compliance and provide more even absorption in the body.

- It may take a month or so for the effects of clonidine to be seen and even more time for optimal effect to be reached. Sudden discontinuation of this medication can cause increased hyperactivity, headache, agitation, elevated blood pressure and pulse, and an increase in tics in patients with Tourette's syndrome.

- Sleepiness, which is the most common side effect of clonidine, gradually decreases after a few weeks. Other side effects may include dry mouth, dizziness, nausea, and light sensitivity. The skin patch can cause a rash.

- Guanfacine is a long-acting noradrenergic agonist similar to clonidine in effect, but it has a longer duration of action and less side-effects. It is used with children who cannot tolerate the sedative effects of clonidine or with children for whom the effects of clonidine were too short.

SSRI Antidepressants

Selective serotonin reuptake inhibitors (SSRIs) are the most commonly used antidepressants for children. These include fluoxetine (Prozac), paroxetine (Paxil), citalopram (Celexa), sertraline (Zoloft), escitalopram (Lexapro), and fluvoxamine (Luvox). These drugs have not been well studied in the treatment of ADHD. SSRIs have, however, gained considerable recognition for treatment of depression, anxiety, and obsessive-compulsive disorders. They are considered the first line of medication treatment for these conditions. They have fewer sedative, cardiovascular, and weight-gain side effects than other antidepressants. The SSRIs are similar in their overall effect of making serotonin available in certain regions of the brain, but they vary somewhat from one another in their chemical make-up. Therefore, when one SSRI proves ineffective for a child, another may be more effective. Parents should be cautious however, about the use of antidepressants in general (including the SSRIs) in children. In October 2003 the FDA issued a health advisory warning doctors to exercise caution in prescribing the SSRIs for children and adolescents and to closely monitor those who take these medications. There are concerns that the SSRIs may increase suicidal ideation or suicide attempts in children and adolescents.

Bupropion (Wellbutrin) is a novel antidepressant drug that has been used successfully for a number of years to treat ADHD. It has not been well studied in this regard, but clinicians using this medication find it has a place in treating ADHD, especially in children who do not tolerate stimulants or who may have co-existing problems with mood. Bupropion appears to possess both indirect dopamine and noradrenergic effects. It works rapidly, peaking in the blood after two hours and lasting up to fourteen hours. The usual dose range in children is from 37.5 to 300 mg per day in two or three divided doses. There is a sustained-release preparation (100, 150, and 200 mg) that can be given once or twice daily. An extended-release form (150 mg and 300 mg) can be given once in the morning. The major side-effects in children are irritability, decreased appetite, insomnia, and worsening of tics. Irritability can be reduced with decreased dosing. Bupropion may worsen tics and should not be used when a seizure disorder is suspected.

Venlafaxine (Effexor) is an antidepressant that, like SSRIs, enhances serotonin in certain areas of the brain by blocking its reuptake, but it also possesses some noradrenergic properties. For this reason it is known as an SNRI (serotonin-norepinephrine reuptake inhibitor). It can improve symptoms of ADHD and is also helpful for depression in children. The usual dose range is 12.5 mg up to a total of 225 mg daily in twice-a-day split dosing. An extended-release (XR) tablet is available allowing once-a-day dosing. Side effects can include nausea, agitation, stomachaches, headaches, and, at higher doses, blood pressure elevation. As with other anti-depressants, there may be a greater risk of suicidally in children and therefore, careful observation of your child while starting this treatment and during the earlier phases of treatment is very important.

Buspirone, an anxiolitic medication, has been used in children and adolescents with anxiety disorders and researchers have reported significant improvement with it. It has not been well studied in the treatment of ADHD in children

Fenfluramine, benzodiazepines, or lithium are of benefit in other psychiatric disorders, but there is no support to their use in the treatment of ADHD.

Antipsychotics

The group of medications called antipsychotics are commonly used to treat disorders other than psychosis and have been found to be very helpful in children who have severe mood lability. They include haloperidol (Haldol), pimozide (Orap), thioridazine (Mellaril), chlorpromazine (Thorazine), and others. They are frequently prescribed to children with severe mood disorders when other medications have failed. Because they have serious side effects, they are reserved for children who show severe problems and who don't respond to other medications. Common short-term, reversible side effects are drowsiness, increased appetite and weight gain, dizziness, dry mouth, congestion, and blurred vision. Some of the antipsychotic drugs can produce side effects that affect various muscle groups (extrapyramidal effects) leading to muscle tightness and spasm, rolling eyes, and restlessness. Some of these severe side effects may be reduced by using the newer, atypical antipsychotics.

Summary

Medications are commonly used to treat people of all ages who have ADHD. We used to think ADHD medications were a treatment of last resort, only to be used after other treatments have been tried and failed, or in children and adolescents who are most severely affected, This is no longer the case. The use of medication is common, generally safe, and very effective for the treatment of ADHD. Results of many controlled studies indicated that medication alone can be very effective to reduce core symptoms of ADHD if dosing is carefully adjusted and monitored.

There are several classes of medications used in the treatment of ADHD. Stimulants are the most frequently used and antidepressants and anti-hypertensives are less often prescribed. There have been many controlled studies of stimulants in the treatment of ADHD. These studies confirm their effectiveness in more than 70 percent of children with improvements noted in attention, activity level, impulsivity, work completion in school, and compliant behavior. New, long-acting stimulants, which can last ten to twelve hours, will eliminate the need for mid-day dosing and may reduce rebound effects.

Antidepressants have been less well studied, but are useful in treating adolescents who do not respond well to the stimulants or who are suffering from depression or low self-esteem in addition to ADHD. The antihypertensive medications have also been less well studied than stimulants and are used to treat those with ADHD who may be very hyperactive, who are aggressive, or who have an accompanying tic disorder. New medications are being tested for treatment of ADHD with some promising results.

When medications are used in treatment, their effects should be monitored. Adjustments in dosage, time taken, or changes in medication type may be made by the physician if problems arise. Parents, teachers, and the adolescent taking the medication should each be responsible for communicating medication effects.

Medication will rarely be the only treatment a child, adolescent, or adult with ADHD receives. A multi-modal treatment program should include counseling, education about ADHD, and school-based or work-based accommodations and interventions.

Chapter 11

Parents as Advocates
Helping Your Child Succeed in School

Parents as Advocates

Most parents of children with ADHD know that negative school reports are inevitable. As a parent, the last thing you want to hear is that your child is having problems in school. Although you've heard it before, its the type of news you never really get used to.

Parents can have different reactions upon hearing about their child's school problems. Some become defensive and angry. Their frustrations may spill over to the school and the teacher, quickly blaming them for their child's difficulties. Other parents avoid the problem, perhaps hoping it will subside on its own or the teacher will find a solution. Still others become discouraged and essentially give up trying to solve their child's unending school problems. Most parents take a more productive stance. They may meet with the teacher and others at school to develop a plan to help the child.

It is in the best interest of your child that you act as an advocate for your child in school. If you don't stand up for your child and make sure your child is receiving an appropriate education, then who will? As an advocate you will need to know about the laws which were written to ensure that your child receives a free and appropriate education. You will also need to know how school systems function and what you, as a spokesperson for your child, can do to bring about changes that will benefit your child.

Your Child's Legal Rights

Getting an appropriate education in our country is a right, not a favor. Laws such as the Rehabilitation Act of 1973, the Individuals with Disabilities Education Act (IDEA) [formerly the Education for All Handicapped Children Act of 1975 (EHA)], and the Americans with Disabilities Act (ADA) exist in our country to protect those with disabling conditions from discrimination and to improve educational and other services available to them. They ensure that disabled persons, regardless of the nature and severity of their disability, be provided a free appropriate public education and that they be educated with non-disabled students to the maximum extent appropriate to their needs. Furthermore, they stipulate that state and local educational agencies must take steps to identify and locate all unserved disabled children and must evaluate such individuals to avoid inappropriate education stemming from misclassification. The laws also require that procedural safeguards be established to enable parents and guardians to have an active say regarding the evaluation and placement of their children in educational program.

Federal Laws Which Protect Students with Disabilities

The Individuals with Disabilities Education Act (IDEA) requires states education agencies to provide appropriate services for disabled children ages birth to 21. To be eligible for special education under IDEA, the child must meet the criteria for eligibility contained in one of the eligibility categories in the law. These categories include serious emotional disturbance, learning disabilities, retardation, traumatic brain injury, autism, vision and hearing impairments, physical disabilities, and other health impairments. If the child meets the criteria of one or more of these categories, requires special education or related services, and his or her disability adversely affects educational performance, the child may be eligible to receive services. Although ADHD is not listed as a specific category of impairment in IDEA, the U.S. Department of Education has made it clear that students with ADHD may qualify for special education or related services under the category of "other health impaired" on the basis of having ADHD alone.

Section 504 of the Rehabilitation Act of 1973 requires public school districts to provide a free, appropriate public education to every "qualified handicapped person" residing within their jurisdiction. The school must conduct an evaluation to determine whether or not the child is "handicapped" as defined by the law. If the child is found to have "a physical or mental impairment, which substantially limits a major life activity (e.g., learning)," then the local education agency must make an "individualized determination of the child's educational needs for regular or special education or related aids or services." The Office of Civil Rights (OCR) is the federal agency within the Department of Education that enforces Section 504. OCR has ruled that ADHD children are "qualified handicapped persons" under Section 504 if their ability to learn or to otherwise benefit from their education is substantially limited due to ADHD.

Section 504 also states that the child's education must be provided in the regular classroom, "unless it is demonstrated that education in the regular environment with the use of supplementary aids and services cannot be achieved satisfactorily." The department encouraged state and local education agencies to take necessary steps to make accommodations within the regular education classroom to meet the needs of students with ADHD. The policy clarification emphasized the important role that teachers in regular education have in providing help to students with ADHD. It also emphasized that steps should be taken to train regular education teachers and other personnel to develop their awareness about ADHD.

The Americans with Disabilities Act of 1990 (ADA) guarantees disabled people access to employment, transportation, telecommunications, public accommodations and public services. The ADA expands on the concepts and protections introduced by Section 504 of the Rehabilitation Act of 1973. It provides comprehensive federal civil rights protections for people with disabilities in the private and public sectors.

IDEA, Section 504, and the ADA all have a similar purpose, to protect disabled persons from discrimination, but they differ in many respects.

On Becoming an Advocate

Federal laws guarantee that your child has the right to a free appropriate education and that you, as a parent, have the right to participate in the educational process to make sure your child receives what s/he is entitled. If the educational process fails to work for your child then it is up to you to make sure this guarantee sticks.

If you bought a stereo and it didn't work you could use the manufacturer's or seller's product guarantee to take action. You would return with proof of purchase and either get it repaired or replaced or your money refunded. You wouldn't wait for the company to call you to see if how you liked their product. You wouldn't sit and complain and do nothing. You would take action. It's the same with the guarantee you have on your child's education.

If you think your child is not receiving an appropriate education you could use your guarantee (laws) to ensure that the school will find out if there is a problem and to provide the right solution (program or services) for your child. However, it is up to you to make sure that these laws are implemented properly. Your child's school will do some of the work for you, but in the end it is up to the parent to monitor the child's process. Parents can become good advocates for their child in school if they understand their legal rights and are willing to voice their concerns to the school when the educational process is not working for their child.

Many parents are reluctant to exercise their legal rights because they feel intimidated by their child's teachers and school administrators. Perhaps this is because as children, most of us were taught to respect our teachers and to revere our principals. We were instructed not to question their authority, to always ask permission before speaking, and to follow their instructions to the letter or risk a poor grade, disapproval or disciplinary action. Given such indoctrination, it is not surprising that as adults it is hard for many parents to overcome their apprehension when they come face-to-face with a teacher or principal and have to question the actions or opinions of the school. This is especially true if your child is having a problem in school.

If your child is a great student, having a parent-teacher conference is a piece of cake. The teacher lavishes one praise after another on your child, tells you that she wishes she had 25 more like him/her in the class, and compliments you on the superb job of parenting you must have done to create such a model citizen. You feel as if you got a straight A report card for being the world's most excellent parent and you leave the conference bursting with pride eager to tell the whole world the great news.

If your child has ADHD, facing the teacher can be more like a nightmare than a dream. Chances are pretty good that you will leave the conference feeling depressed, demoralized, and defeated, the result of listening to a long litany of complaints about your son or daughter that you have heard many times before. You might feel as if you are to blame, that if only you were a better parent, spent more time checking his schoolwork, didn't let him get away with things as much, were a better example for him to follow, etc. he wouldn't have as many problems. Guilt, shame and embarrassment can set in and you may be apologizing for your child, promising to take immediate action to remedy the situation, and pledging unending support and cooperation to the teacher.

To be an effective advocate, it is important that parents:
1. know about their child's disability and how it affects their education;
2. understand the system of laws that exist to protect students with disabilities;
3. be familiar with how schools function and the steps that are involved in accessing appropriate services; and
4. communicate effectively with others.

149

Open-Minded versus Close-Minded Schools

Every parent is their child's first teacher. As such, parents usually have a good understanding how their child thinks and learns and can offer vital information to the school to help their child in the educational process. Depending on the willingness of the school a parent's ideas may be heartily welcomed or flatly ignored. When communicating their ideas the parent may be meeting with the child's teacher alone or in a group with other members of the school's faculty such as the guidance counselor, exceptional education specialist, school psychologist, department chairperson, etc. Just as parents and teachers vary in their personality, schools and teams also vary in their attitude toward parents and their receptivity to parental communication.

Open-minded school systems (teachers, teams) recognize the vital role that parents play in the educational process. They seek to form partnership relationships with parents knowing that a cooperative parent often makes their job of teaching more enjoyable and productive. Open-minded schools encourage parents to express their ideas, communicate frequently with parents about their child, and when problems come up work together with the parents to formulate solutions and to monitor progress. Obviously parents find it much easier to communicate their ideas in such a setting. They feel as if they are a part of the process of educating their child and are likely to volunteer time and energy in working more closely with the child in the educational process.

Close-minded schools (teachers, teams) tend to be education "know-it-alls." They are difficult for parents to approach and take on a stern, rigid, and judgemental attitude when communicating with parents. Close-minded school systems tend to discredit what parents say and place more value on what they see than on information from other sources. Parents frequently avoid communication under such circumstances or become defensive, hostile and uncooperative. They often leave meetings feeling intimidated, angry and discouraged.

Who is responsible for these different attitudes? Sometimes the tone a school has is set by the school's administrator. Sometimes one or two teachers on a team can create a negative or positive tone. In some cases, the parent may be the one who creates a negative tone, acting hostile, defensive or judgemental when dealing with the school.

Parent Empowerment

Parents need to be empowered to advocate for their children in school. Empowerment enables people to obtain the knowledge, skills, and abilities necessary to make their own decision and gain control of their own lives. Empowerment is a natural process which often begins when you first learn that your child has a disability. Fearful that their child will not succeed in school, it is no wonder that many parents strive to gain some control over their child's schooling both to assist and to protect their child. If you are one of these parents, you are not alone. And if there is courage in numbers, then you should have plenty to spare, because there are hundreds of thousands of parents of children with ADHD who are feeling the same frustrations you are and who are learning to change, not just accept, the way schools currently educate their children.

Empowered Parents
- are motivated by the fact their child has a disability
- act on motivation by identifying resources and vowing to find others
- are proactive
- opt for the right path for the child even if it is more difficult
- make a powerful impact for themselves and others

Non-empowered Parents
- are not motivated
- accept things as they are and don't try to change things
- are reactive, not proactive
- choose path of least resistance
- make very little difference in their family's life (much less in the lives of other families)

151

How the Process Works
Step 1: The Referral

If your child has been identified as having problems in school which suggest that he might be disabled and in need of special education services, the rules and regulations of your local and state school system require that a referral be made to determine whether the child is indeed disabled and what kind of special education programming and related services might be needed to educate him appropriately. This process begins with a written referral to the principal of the school the child is in or would attend if he were in a public school. Any of your child's teachers can make such a referral, or you can as well if you think your child needs special education services.

After the referral is made, the principal will call a committee meeting to consider the referral. Committee members usually include the child's teacher(s), the person making the referral, other specialists involved with the child or the school, the principal or someone designated by the principal. The name given to this initial committee varies from district to district, but is sometimes referred to a the "school screening committee," "child study team," "educational management team," etc. The committee's purpose is to review your child's progress in school, to assess his/her learning and school performance and to determine whether these problems warrant a formal evaluation by the school psychologist or other specialist. Prior to obtaining such an evaluation the committee might gather data from other sources, may make suggestions about adapting the child's current school program to better meet the needs of the child, or may suggest strategies to the classroom teacher that might help the child. If members of the committee recommend that the child receive a full evaluation, the child may be referred to a school psychologist or other specialist for that purpose. You must be informed in writing of the committee's decision.

Depending on the district, parents may not even be aware that their child has been referred to the committee for consideration. Some districts are careful to notify the parents of any meetings held to make a decision about a child's educational needs, others only notify the parent if they want to obtain your consent for a formal evaluation. Whether you are invited or not to this meeting, if you are aware that your child is being referred to the committee for consideration you should contact the school and ask to be involved in this initial meeting. If the screening committee does not recommend that your child receive an evaluation you can dispute this decision through a formal procedure called a due process hearing. Due process procedures will be discussed later.

If you had not had prior knowledge of the committee meeting, the first you might hear of it is when you receive a letter requesting your permission for the school to evaluate your child. The school must notify you of its wish to evaluate your child for purposes of receiving special education services. It must review with you what the purpose of the evaluation is and what tests will be administered to your child. Before any testing can begin, the school must have your consent. If you refuse to give consent, the school system must initiate a due process hearing and have a hearing officer rule to proceed with the evaluation.

Step 2: The Evaluation

The purpose of the evaluation is to determine whether the student has a disability and the student's educational needs. School districts across the country often differ in how they initially evaluate students with ADHD. Some do a full comprehensive assessment following the procedures outlined in IDEA to determine whether a student qualifies for special education or related services. Others do briefer assessments, seeking to determine whether a student qualifies for a 504 Plan.

Under IDEA it is required that the evaluation be conducted by a multi-disciplinary team of professionals with expertise in different areas. These evaluations are usually quite comprehensive in scope and include assessment of more than one of the following areas: academic achievement, medical tests or reports, social history, psychological testing, speech and language development, tests of hearing and vision. Information from parents, teachers, and other sources is obtained.

Under Section 504, the guidelines for doing evaluations are broader than under IDEA. The evaluation must draw on information from a variety of sources in the area of concern. Many school districts have procedures to do 504 evaluations for students suspected of having ADHD. A full, comprehensive psychoeducational evaluation may not be done as required under IDEA.

Step 3: Determining Eligibility

After the evaluation is completed the committee meets to determine whether the student has a disability and is eligible for protections and programs under federal law.

Step 4: Determining a Program of Services

If it has been decided that the student has a disability, the committee decides whether a 504 Plan or and Individualized Education Program (IEP) would be appropriate to meet the student's needs. This decisions should be based solely on the needs of the student and whether these needs could be met in regular education or special education and the related services that might be necessary.

Step 5: Due Process Procedures

Both IDEA and Section 504 provide a due process mechanism to protect the child from being denied appropriate services. An impartial third party, called a hearing officer, examines the issues on which the parent and the school system disagree and arrives at an unbiased decision.

Writing a 504 Plan

If a student is determined eligible to receive services under Section 504, a 504 Plan must be written. This plan must be designed to meet the individual educational needs of the student. The 504 Plan lists the accommodations (i.e., specialized instruction or equipment, auxiliary aids or services, program modifications, etc.) the committee recommends as necessary to ensure the student's access to all district programs.

Most students with 504 Plans are receiving accommodations within the regular education classroom. Examples of such accommodations can be found below. A case manager is assigned to monitor the student's progress under the plan. Future meetings between the parents and committee members should be scheduled to review the student's progress and the effectiveness of the plan.

Below is a list of accommodations that can be put on a 504 Plan to accommodate students with ADHD.

Assignments/Worksheets
- extra time to complete tasks
- simplify directions
- hand worksheets one at a time
- shorten assignments
- allow use of word processor
- use self-monitor devices
- provide training in study skills
- break work into small parts
- allow use of tape recorder
- don't grade handwriting

Behaviors
- praise specific behaviors
- use self-monitoring devices or programs
- give extra privileges/rewards
- cue students to stay on task
- increase immediacy of rewards
- mark correct answers not incorrect ones
- use classroom behavior management program
- allow legitimate movement
- allow student time out of seat to run errands
- ignore minor, inappropriate behavior
- use time-out procedure for misbehavior
- seat student near good role model
- set up behavior contract
- ignore calling out without raising hand
- praise student when hand raised

Lesson Presentation
- pair students to check work
- write major points on chalkboard
- ask student to repeat instructions
- use computer assisted instruction
- break longer presentations into shorter ones
- provide written outline
- make frequent eye contact with student
- include a variety of activities during each lesson

Physical Arrangement of Room
- seat student near teacher
- seat student near positive role model
- avoid distracting stimuli (window, air conditioner noise, etc.)
- increase distance between desks
- stand near student when giving directions

Organization
- provide peer assistance with organizational skills
- assign volunteer homework buddy
- allow student to have an extra set of books at home
- send daily/weekly progress notes home for parents
- provide homework assignment book
- review rules of neatness on written assignments
- help student organize materials in desk/backpack,
- develop reward system for completion of classwork/homework
- teach time management principles
- help student organize long-term projects by setting shorter goals

Test Taking
- allow open book exams
- give exams orally if written language is difficult
- give take home tests
- use more objective tests as opposed to essays
- allow student to give test answers on tape recorder
- allow extra time for tests

Academic Skill
- if skill weaknesses are suspected refer for academic achievement assessment

- if reading is weak: provide previewing strategies; select text with less on a page; shorten amount of required reading
- if oral expression is weak: accept all oral responses; substitute display for oral report; encourage expression of new ideas; pick topics that are easy for student to talk about
- if written language is weak: accept non-written forms for reports; accept use of typewriter, word processor, tape recorder; do not assign large quantity of written work; give multiple choice tests rather than essay tests
- if math is weak: allow use of calculator; use graph paper to space numbers; provide additional math time; provide immediate correctness feedback and instruction via modeling of the correct computational procedure; teach steps to solve type of math problem; encourage use of "self-talk" to proceed through problem solving

Special Considerations
- alert bus driver to needs of student
- suggest parenting program
- monitor closely on field trips
- communicate with physician regarding effects of medication and other treatments the student may be receiving
- suggest other agency involvement as needed
- social skills training
- counseling
- establish procedure for dispensing medication
- consult with other outside professionals, i.e., counselor
- monitor medication side-effects

The Individualized Education Program (IEP)

If the student is deemed eligible to receive special education under IDEA, he must have an Individualized Education Program (IEP) designed specifically to meet his needs. The IEP is at the heart of the whole process of special education because it specifies the services and programs that the adolescent will receive as a result of his disability. It is the school's commitment that a student will receive specific programs and services. The IEP is individualized in that it meets the student's unique identified educational needs rather than those of the group.

The IEP specifies the educational placement or setting in which the student will receive instruction, lists specific goals and educational objectives for your child to reach, and designates the related services that your child will receive to enable him to reach those goals and objectives. The IEP also contains dates when services will begin, how long they will last, and the method by which your child's progress will be evaluated. The IEP will be reviewed periodically and modifications will be made as needed.

The 1997 IDEA amendments added some new requirements in the development of IEPs, which are of particular concern to students with ADHD. The IEP team must consider the strengths of the child and the concerns of the parents for enhancing the education of their child. The IEP must take into account the results of the initial evaluation and most recent evaluation of the child In the case of a child whose behavior impedes his or her learning or that of others, the IEP must take into account the appropriate strategies, including positive behavioral interventions and strategies that address this behavior.

The 1997 IDEA amendments also promote the inclusion of disabled students and requires statements in the IEP concerning how the child's disability affects the child's involvement and progress in the general curriculum.

Summary

Parents and teachers play important roles as advocates for children with disabilities. To be an effective advocate, they need to have an understanding of how the student's disability affects educational performance and what laws exist to protect disabled students. Federal laws such as IDEA, Section 504 of the Rehabilitation Act of 1973, and the Americans with Disabilities Act of 1990 ensure protections for children with disabilities. These laws differ in terms of how they each define who is eligible for such programs and services, how evaluations should be conducted to determine such eligibility, procedures for providing services, and safeguards for parents and guardians upon which to rely.

If a student is deemed eligible to receive services based on a disability, either a 504 Plan or an Individualized Education Program (IEP) will be written. These documents specify the services that will be provided to the student. Parents who disagree with any of the findings of the school can follow due process procedures to file grievances.

Chapter 12

Communicating with Parents

To be successful teaching a student with ADHD, teachers must work closely with the student's parents. This close cooperation and communication will serve to keep both parties informed as to the student's needs. Changes in medication may require more careful monitoring by the teacher. Changes in assignments given for homework may require the parent to more closely supervise the student's work. Behavior problems may be reduced with a daily report card system or a school-based contingency program that is supported by the child's parents.

Below are a list of considerations teachers should keep in mind when communicating with parents:

- Put yourself in the shoes of the parent and try to understand what they have been through with their child.

- At the beginning of the school year, make the first contact with the parents to introduce yourself and to assure the parents you will be available to them. Be encouraging and positive.

- Do not assume that the student's problems are the fault of the parents, either because of poor parenting skills, neglect, or abuse. The parents may have tried everything they knew of to help their child, but problems still persist. Discuss the different treatments the child has received to better understand what has been tried and what has helped.

161

- Do not judge or blame the parent for the student's problems. Offer understanding and assistance.

- Communicate frequently with parents and try to make the feedback as positive as you can. Always find something positive to communicate while dealing with the problems as well.

- Continue to inspire hope in the parents that their child can do better. A parent who is discouraged may give up, making your work with the student much harder and the likelihood of the student succeeding much lower.

- Advise parents that the school district has policies regarding the rights of children with disabilities and that children with ADHD may be eligible for special education services or accommodations.

- Find out if the student has a 504 Plan. Discuss it with the parents and other teachers. Implement the plan and monitor carefully to determine its effectiveness.

- Help parents form appropriate expectations about their child.

- Do not recommend that the ADHD child be prescribed medication. This is a medical decision and should be left up to the child's physician. However, if the child is taking medication for ADHD it will be quite helpful if you offer to communicate with the child's doctors about the child's classroom performance.

- Encourage parents to participate in a parent support group. Children and Adults with Attention Deficit Hyperactivity Disorder (CHADD) and the National Attention Deficit Disorder Association (ADDA) are two national groups.

Local chapters of CHADD exist in many communities across the country. For specific locations of a chapter in your area refer to the CHADD web site: www.chadd.org.

- Parents of a newly diagnosed child may need time to accept the diagnosis. Some parents will feel very relieved to have such a diagnosis as it serves to explain their child's problems. Others may resist the diagnosis. Try to understand the parents' reactions to a diagnosis without judging them. Give the parents time to sort things out or to get other opinions.

- When conferencing with parents find out about strategies they use at home to help the student. Perhaps similar strategies applied at school could also help.

- Direct the parent to other community agencies or groups that may have programs to help the family.

- Do not put yourself "above" the parent. Many have had a great deal of experience and education about ADHD and can be a valuable resource for you.

Summary

Teachers are responsible for communicating to parents about the performance of the students in their class. Students with disabilities often benefit when their teachers and parents communicate frequently. Teachers should be sensitive to the struggles that both their students and their students' parents face. Avoid judging either the student or the parent. Teachers should not assume that the student's problems are the fault of the parents. Try to inspire hope in the parents and find positive aspects of the student's school work. Encourage parents to participate in support groups and direct them to other community agencies which may be appropriate.

National Organizations and Resources

National Organizations

American Occupational Therapy Association
4720 Montgomery Lane
Bethesda, MD 20814
(301) 652-2682
www.aota.org

American Speech-Language-Hearing Association
10801 Rockville Pike
Rockville, MD 20852
(800) 638-8255
www.asha.org

Association on Higher Education and Disability (AHEAD)
P.O. Box 21192
Columbus, OH 43221-0192
(614) 488-4972

Attention Deficit Disorders Association (ADDA)
P.O. Box 1303
Northbrook, IL 60065
(216) 350-9595
www.adda.org

Children and Adults with Attention Deficit Hyperactivity Disorder (CHADD)
8181 Professional Drive, Suite 202
Lanham, MD 20706
(800) 233-4050
www.chadd.org

Council for Exceptional Children
Eric Clearinghouse on Disabilities and Education
1920 Association Drive
Reston, VA 20191
(800) 328-0272
www.cec.sped.org

Learning Disabilities Association of America (LDAA)
4156 Library Road
Pittsburgh, PA 15234
(412) 341-1515
www.ldanatl.org

National Information Center for Children and Youth with Disabilities (NICHCY)
P.O. Box 1492
Washington, DC 20013-1492
(800) 695-0285
www.nichcy.org

Recordings for the Blind and Dyslexic
20 Roszel Road
Princeton, NJ 08540
(800) 221-4792

Tourette Syndrome Association
4240 Bell Blvd.
Bayside, NY 11361
(718) 224-2999

165

Resources for Books, Videos, Training, and Assessment Products

A.D.D. WareHouse
300 N. W. 70th Ave., Suite 102
Plantation, Florida 33317
(800) 233-9273 • (954) 792-8100
www.addwarehouse.com

American Guidance Service
4201 Woodland Road
Circle Pines, MN 55014
(800) 328-2560
www.agsnet.com

Boys Town Press
14100 Crawford Street
Boys Town, NE 68010
(800) 282-6657
www.ffbh.boystown.org

Childswork/Childsplay
135 Dupont St.
P.O. Box 760
Plainview, NY 11803-0760
(800) 962-1141
www.childswork.com

Educational Resource Specialists
P.O. Box 19207
San Diego, CA 92159
(800) 682-3528

Franklin Electronic Publishers Inc.
One Franklin Plaza
Burlington, NJ 08016
(800) 525-9673

Free Spirit Publishing
400 First Ave. North, Suite 616
Minneapolis, MN 55401
(800) 735-7323
www.freespirit.com

Gordon Systems, Inc.
P.O. Box 746
DeWitt, N.Y. 13214-746
(315) 446-4849

Guilford Publications
72 Spring St.
New York, New York, 10012
(800) 365-7006
www.guilford.com

Hawthorne Educational Services
800 Gray Oak Drive
Columbia, MO 65201
(800) 542-1673

MHS
908 Niagara Falls Blvd.
North Tonawanda, NY 14120
(800) 456-3003
www.mhs.com

Neurology, Learning and Behavior
Center
230 500 East, Suite 100
Salt Lake City, UT 84102
(801) 532-1484

PCI Educational Publishing
12029 Warfield
San Antonio, TX 78216
(800) 594-4263
www.pcicatalog.com

Prentice Hall/Center for Applied
Research in Education
200 Old Tappan Road
Old Tappan, NJ 07675
(800) 922-0579

Slosson Educational Publications
P.O. Box 280
East Aurora, NY 14052
(888) 756-7766
www.slosson.com

Sopris West
P.O. Box 1809
Longmont, CO 80502-1809
(800) 547-6747
www.sopriswest.com

Western Psychological Services
Creative Therapy Store
12031 Wilshire Blvd.
Los Angeles, CA 90025
(800) 648-8857

Suggested Books and Videos

Books and Training Programs for Teachers and Parents

Alexander-Roberts, C. (1995). *ADHD and teens: A parent's guide to making it through the tough years.* Dallas, TX: Taylor Publishing Co.

Barkley, R.A. (2005). *Attention deficit hyperactivity disorder: A handbook for diagnosis and treatment (3rd Edition).* New York: Guilford Press.

Barkley, R. A. & Benton, C. M. (1998). *Your defiant child. Eight steps to better behavior.* New York: Guilford Press.

Barkley, R. A. (1995). *Taking charge of ADHD: The complete authoritative guide for parents.* New York: Guilford Press.

Bowman, L. (1995). *Pay attention! Stop, think & listen: A self-monitoring program for classroom and home behavior management.* Plantation, FL: Specialty Press, Inc.

Bramer, J. S. (1996). *Succeeding in college with attention deficit disorders: Issues and strategies for students, counselors, and educators.* Plantation, FL: Specialty Press, Inc.

Cumine, V., Leach, J., & Stevenson, G. (1998). *Asperger syndrome. A practical guide for teachers.* London: David Fulton Publishers.

Dendy, C.A. (2002). *Teaching teens with ADD and ADHD.* Maryland: Woodbine House.

Dendy, C. A. (1995). *Teenagers with ADD: A parents' guide.* Maryland: Woodbine House.

DuPaul, G. & Stoner, G. (1994). *ADHD in the schools: Assesment and intervention strategies.* New York: Guilford Press.

Fellman, W. R. (1997). *The other me: Poetic thoughts on ADD for adults, kids, and parents.* Plantation, FL: Specialty Press, Inc.

Flick, G. L. (1998). *ADD/ADHD Behavior-change resource kit*: West Nyack, NY: The Center for Applied Research in Education.

Fowler, M. C. (1992). *CH.A.D.D. educators manual*. Plantation, FL: CH.A.D.D.

Goldstein, S. & Goldstein, M. (1992). *Hyperactivity: Why won't my child pay attention?* Salt Lake City, UT: Neurology, Learning and Behavior Center.

Goldstein, S. & Mathers, N. (1998). *Overcoming underachievement: An action guide to helping your child succeed in school*. New York: John Wiley & Sons.

Gordon, M. (1991). *ADHD/hyperactivity: A consumer's guide*. DeWitt, NY: GSI Publications.

Gordon, M. (1989). *Attention training system*. DeWitt, NY: Gordon Systems.

Hagar, K., Goldstein, S., Brooks, R. (2006). *Seven steps to improve your child's social skills*. Plantation, FL: Specialty Press, Inc.

Hallowell, E. H. & Ratey, J. (2005). *Delivered from distraction*. New York: Random House.

Hallowell, E. H. (1996). *When you worry about the child you love: Emotional and learning problems in children*. New York: Simon and Schuster.

Hallowell, E. & Ratey, J. (1994). *Driven to distraction*. New York: Simon and Schuster.

Ingersoll, B. & Goldstein, S. (1993). *Attention deficit disorders and learning disabilities: Realities, myths, and controversial treatments*. New York: Doubleday.

Koplewicz, H. S. (1996). *It's nobody's fault: New hope and help for difficult children and their parents*. New York: Random House.

Latham P., & Latham, P. (1998). *ADD and the law* (2nd ed.). Washington, DC: JKL Communications.

March, J. S. & Mulle, K. (1998). *OCD in children and adolescents. A cognitive-behavioral treatment manual.* New York: Guilford Press.

Mannix, D. (1998). *Social skills activities for secondary students with special needs.* New York: The Center for Applied Research in Education.

Nadeau, K. G. & Biggs, S. H. (1995). *School strategies for ADD teens.* VA: Chesapeake Psychological Services.

Papolos, D. F. & Papolos, J. (1999). *The bipolar child.* New York: Broadway Books.

Parker, H. C. (2005). *The ADHD workbook for parents.* Plantation, FL: Specialty Press, Inc.

Parker, H. C. (2005). *The ADHD handbook for schools.* Plantation, FL: Specialty Press, Inc.

Parker, H. C. (1999). *Put yourself in their shoes: Understanding teenagers with attention deficit hyperactivity disorder.* Plantation, FL: Specialty Press, Inc.

Parker, H.C. (1992). *ADAPT: Attention deficit accommodation plan for teaching.* Plantation, FL: Specialty Press, Inc.

Parker, H. C. (1991). *The goal card program.* Plantation, FL: Specialty Press, Inc.

Parker, H. C. (1990). *Listen, look, and think.* Plantation, FL: Specialty Press, Inc.

Partin, R. (1995). *Classroom teacher's survival guide.* New York: The Center for Applied Research in Education.

Pennington, B. F. (1991). *Diagnosing learning disorders: A neuropsychological framework.* New York: Guilford Press.

Pfiffner, L. J. (1996). *All about ADHD: The complete practical guide for classroom teachers.* New York: Scholastic, Inc.

Phelan, T. (2003). *1-2-3 Magic: Effective Discipline for Children 2-12 (3rd Edition).* Glen Ellyn, Illinois: ParentMagic, Inc.

Phelan, T. (1993). *Surviving your adolescents.* Glenn Elyn: IL: Child Management.

Rhode, G., Jenson, W. R., & Reavis, H. K. (1995). *The tough kid tool box*. Longmont, CO: Sopris West

Rief, S. (2005). *How to reach and teach children with ADD/ ADHD. (2nd Edition)*. New York: Jossey Bass.

Rief, S. (1998). *The ADD/ADHD checklist*. Paramus, NJ: Prentice Hall.

Rief, S. (1993). *How to reach and teach ADD/ADHD children*. West Nyack, NY: The Center for Applied Research in Education.

Shapiro, E. S. & Kratochwill, T. R. (2000). *Conducting school-based assessments of child and adolescent behavior*. New York: Guilford Press.

Silver, L. (1993). *Dr. Larry Silver's advice to parents on attention-deficit hyperactivity disorder*. Washington, DC: American Psychiatric Press.

Sirotowitz, S., Davis, L., & Parker, H. (2004). *Study Ssrategies for early school success*. Plantation: FL: Specialty Press, Inc.

Thompson, J. G. (1998). *Discipline survival kit for the secondary teacher*. West Nyack, NY: The Center for Applied Research in Education.

Wender, P. H. (1987). *The hyperactive child, adolescent, and adult*. New York: Oxford Press.

Videos for Teachers and Parents

Barkley, R. A. (1992). *ADHD—What do we know?* New York: The Guilford Press.

Barkley, R. A. (1992). *ADHD—What can we do?* New York: The Guilford Press.

Barkley, R. A. (1992). *ADHD in adults*. New York: The Guilford Press.

Barkley, R. A. (1997). *Understanding defiant behavior*. New York: The Guilford Press.

Barkley, R. A. (1997). *Managing defiant behavior*. New York: The Guilford Press.

Biederman, J., Spencer, T., & Wilens, T. (1997). *Medical management of attention deficit hyperactivity disorder—parts I and II.* Plantation, FL: Specialty Press, Inc.

Bramer, J. S. & Fellman, W. (1997). *Success in college and career with attention deficit disorders.* Plantation, FL: Specialty Press, Inc.

Brooks, R. (1997). *Look what you've done! Learning disabilities and self-esteem: stories of hope and resilience.* Washington, D.C.: WETA.

Lavoie, R. (2005). *It's so much work to be your friend: Helping the child with learning disabilities find social success.* New York: Simon & Schuster.

Lavoie, R. (1990). *How difficult can this be? The F.A.T. city workshop.* Washington, DC: WETA.

Phelan, T. *1-2-3 Magic! Training your preschooler and preteen to do what you want them to do!* Glen Ellyn, IL: Child Management, Inc.

Robin, A. L. & Weiss, S. K. (1997). *Managing oppositional youth. Effective, practical strategies for managing the behavior of hard to manage kids and teens!* Plantation, FL: Specialty Press, Inc.

Sheridan, S. (1997). *Why don't they like me? Helping your child make and keep friends.* Longmont, CO: Sopris West.

Waltz, M. (2000). Bipolar disorders. A guide to helping children and adolescents. Cambridge: O'Reilly.

Zentall, S. S. & Goldstein, S. (1999). *Seven steps to homework success: A family guide for solving common homework problems.* Plantation, FL: Specialty Press, Inc.

Books and Videos for Children and Adolescents

Bramer, J. S. (1996). *Succeeding in college with attention deficit disorders: Issues and strategies for students, counselors, & educators.* Plantation, FL: Specialty Press, Inc.

Bramer, J. S. & Fellman, W. (1997). *Success in college and career with attention deficit disorders.* Plantation, FL: Specialty Press, Inc. (Video)

Corman, C. & Trevino, E. *Eukee the jumpy jumpy elephant.* Plantation, FL: Specialty Press, Inc.

Davis, L., Sirotowitz, S. & Parker, H. (1996). *Study strategies made easy: A practical plan for school success.* Plantation, FL: Specialty Press, Inc.

Davis, L., & Sirotowitz, S. (1997). *Study strategies made easy: A practical plan for school success.* Plantation, FL: Specialty Press, Inc. (Video)

Gehret, J. (1990). *Eagle eyes: A child's view of attention deficit disorder.* Fairport, NY: Verbal Images Press.

Goldstein, S. & Goldstein, M. (1991). *It's just attention disorder: A video for kids.* Salt Lake City, UT: Neurology, Learning and Behvior Center. (Video)

Gordon, M. (1993). *I would if I could: A teenager's guide to ADHD/Hyperactivity.* DeWitt, NY: GSI Publications.

Gordon, M. (1991). *Jumpin' Johnny get back to work: A child's guide to ADHD/hyperactivity.* DeWitt, NY: GSI Publications.

Nadeau, K. G. & Biggs, S. H. (1993). *School strategies for ADD teens.* Annandale, VA: Chesapeake Psychological Pub.

Nadeau, K. G. (1994). *Survival guide for college students with ADD or LD.* Washington, DC: Magination Press.

Parker, R. N. & Parker, H. C. (1995). *Slam dunk: A young boy's struggle with ADD.* Plantation, FL: Specialty Press, Inc.

Parker, R. N. and Parker, H. C. (1992). *Making the grade: An adolescent's struggle with attention deficit disorders.* Plantation, FL: Specialty Press, Inc.

Quinn, P. O. (1994). *ADD and the college student.* Washington, DC: Magination Press.

Quinn, P. O. & Stern, J. (1991). *Putting on the brakes.* New York: Magination Press.

Index

Symbols